"A deeply rich and spiritual book ⟨...⟩ *and the Life of Faith* offers both church and academy a gift in its wonderful desire not to prize apart speech about God, creation, the church, and the life of the believer. This book is a must for any pastor or theologian."

—**Tom Greggs, FRSE**, University of Aberdeen

"From the glory of God to the glory of an everyday smile—this book draws the reader into renewed praise, more prayerful theology, greater ecumenism, and deeper appreciation of how fundamental glorification is to Scripture, creed, and the Christian life. So it's well worth taking the time to read, learn, and inwardly digest."

—**Frances Young**, University of Birmingham

"This short book takes a deep and wide view of the landscape of God's glory—from the mystery and wonder of the divine life as Trinity, to the glory hidden yet revealed in Jesus, to finding glory in prayer, the simple tasks of life, or the joy of a smile. It is a book worth pondering slowly and carefully as it unfolds a world of glory beyond our imagining."

—**Bishop Graham Tomlin**, Centre for Cultural Witness,
Lambeth Palace

"After centuries of neglect, theology has turned to God's glory as a central and crucial aspect of its dogmatic task. This renaissance is reflected and extended in *Glorification and the Life of Faith*. This book is written to be relished, reflecting its own core recommendation of doxological reading; its promise is fully realized when it attracts the reader to the contemplation of God and God's glory, becoming more fully alive to God, others, and oneself in the process."

—**Jason A. Fout**, Bexley Seabury Seminary

"This book is a blessing, bringing 'respairing joy' and a smile to anyone who takes the time to read, reflect, and pray through its insights. Cocksworth and Ford offer a re-enchantment of creation, church, and our own lives of faith through their powerful evocation of God's glory. In a time when technique, urgency, injustice, and scarcity mindsets threaten us with despair, their beautiful description of glorification and the life of faith calls us to overflowing abundance in praise of God."

—**L. Gregory Jones**, Belmont University

GLORIFICATION
AND THE
LIFE OF FAITH

SOTERIOLOGY AND DOXOLOGY

Kent Eilers and Kyle C. Strobel, Series Editors

Glorification and the Life of Faith
by Ashley Cocksworth and David F. Ford

GLORIFICATION
AND THE
LIFE OF FAITH

Ashley Cocksworth and David F. Ford

Baker Academic
a division of Baker Publishing Group
Grand Rapids, Michigan

Published by Baker Academic
a division of Baker Publishing Group
Grand Rapids, Michigan
www.bakeracademic.com

Printed in the United States of America

Library of Congress Cataloging-in-Publication Data
Names: Cocksworth, Ashley, author. | Ford, David F., 1948– author.
Title: Glorification and the life of faith / Ashley Cocksworth and David F. Ford.
Description: Grand Rapids, Michigan : Baker Academic, a division of Baker Publishing Group,
    [2023] | Series: Soteriology and doxology | Includes bibliographical references and indexes.
Identifiers: LCCN 2023010925 | ISBN 9781540961686 (paperback) | ISBN 9781540966759
    (casebound) | ISBN 9781493442614 (ebook) | ISBN 9781493442621 (pdf)
Subjects: LCSH: Glory of God—Christianity. | Faith (Christianity) | Theology. | Public
    worship.
Classification: LCC BT180.G6 C64 2023 | DDC 234—dc23/eng/20230531
LC record available at https://lccn.loc.gov/2023010925

Baker Publishing Group publications use paper produced from sustainable forestry practices and post-consumer waste whenever possible.

23   24   25   26   27   28   29   7   6   5   4   3   2   1

For Lucy, Maisie, Edna, Julie

For Solomon, Azalea, Josiah, Jack, June

For George and Mira

Contents

Series Preface

And Moses said, "Here I am."

Exodus 3:4

IN THE WILDERNESS, Moses stumbles upon a burning bush that somehow goes unconsumed. As if the scene is not arresting enough, the God of his forefathers bellows forth from that crackling, glowing bush: "Moses, Moses!" The response of Moses is simple and yet so evocative of a faithful response to God's call: "Here I am." Holy Scripture pictures that response time and again. So many other encounters with God are unmistakably echoed and foreshadowed here: Samuel, Mary, Jesus, and of course Adam. To Adam, God calls, "Where are you?" and he hides, and his hiding is paradigmatic of us all, sadly (Gen. 3:8–10); *but* Moses, Samuel, Mary, and Jesus *offer themselves* in response to the gracious calling of God: "Here I am, Lord." Their proclamation inspires what this series humbly attempts to accomplish: theological activity that bears witness to God's work in time and space to redeem and restore by following the doxological pattern of Moses. Addressed by God and fearful to look upon God's face, Moses finds himself suddenly shoeless in God's holy presence.

Said more formally, the volumes in the Soteriology and Doxology series offer specifically theological interpretations of the Christian life through the lens of various features of God's gracious activity to save in which doctrinal activity is suffused with and held together by praise. The

gracious acts of God are the contemplative aim of the series, advancing
Christian rationality in grateful response to the redemptive, restorative,
and transformative work of the Father by the Son and the Spirit. Focusing
on soteriological loci, the topics addressed follow a twofold inclination:
that God is the ever-present, captivating reality of all theological work,
and that this focus awakens a doxological response that is intrinsic to the
proper mode of theological reflection. As such, the orientation of each
volume is both dogmatic *and* doxological: each particular doctrine is lo-
cated within an attentive retrieval of the Christian confession, all while
demonstrating how theological reflection springs from worship and spills
over into prayer and praise. Seeking to be catholic and evangelical, this
series draws upon the richness of the whole church while keeping the
sufficiency and singularity of the gospel at center.

The books in the series are designed for theologians-in-formation,
meaning that the pedagogical aim of each volume is to train student-
readers in a form of theological reasoning that unites what often remains
painfully separate in Christian theology: doctrine and spirituality,
theology and prayer, the church and the academy, the body of Christ and
the individual theologian. This series' approach to theology is exemplified by men and women across the Christian tradition, from Athanasius
to Benedict, Ephrem the Syrian to Anselm, Bonaventure to Catherine of
Sienna, and Aquinas to Calvin. However, with the inclusion of theology
in the academic disciplines of the modern university, the expectations
and norms of theological reasoning have been altered in many quarters:
exegesis is sequestered from theology, and dogmatics from doxology. This
series offers something different. It seeks to retrieve forms of theological
reflection unapologetic about their home within Christian worship and
celebratory of their place within the entire Christian tradition.

With the sight of God as the proper aim of theological contemplation—
trembling before the descending fire that calls us to bear witness to his
presence—each volume seeks to constructively articulate soteriological
loci through the broad range of biblical, historical, and contemporary
issues with an eye to expositing the Christian life. While the different
authors will vary in how they approach these tasks, the overall flow of
each volume will follow a broad fivefold movement: (1) creed, (2) scriptural range, (3) comparative soteriology, (4) constructive theology, and
(5) the Christian life, along with a doxological prelude and doxological

interludes throughout the volumes. Having approached the doctrine from the standpoint of the *regula fidei* through creedal reflection; looked to Holy Scripture for the doctrine's content, scope, and form; and measured diverse traditions of biblical interpretation and theological reasoning, each volume offers a contemporary restatement of Christian teaching that shows how this theological locus directs doxology and Christian living. The *lived* reality of Christian existence, often far from the purview of theological reflection, remains the focused end of articulating the saving acts of God.

> O the depth of the riches and wisdom and knowledge of God! . . . For from him and through him and to him are all things. To him be the glory forever! Amen. (Rom. 11:33, 36)

Kent Eilers
Kyle C. Strobel
Series Editors

Acknowledgments

ALTHOUGH MOST OF THIS BOOK has been written during the pandemic, and therefore has not enjoyed the same sort of academic sociality books written in other times might experience, we have managed to accumulate a sizable debt of gratitude to several groups and individuals over the course of its development.

We owe our greatest debt to our families. At the start of the first wave of the pandemic, I (Ash) became a father for the first time. Lucy has been a constant source of joy and smiles; so too Hannah, the most loving mother and partner, and to whom I owe so much. Then, joy upon joy, Maisie was born during the final stages of this book's production, bringing yet more joy and smiles into our lives. My own father, Christopher, always wise and supportive, has engaged constructively with most of the ideas discussed in this book and has helped make them better—for this, and much more, I am grateful.

Since the conception of this book, I (David) have had the wonderful experience of becoming a grandfather three times over—to Solomon, Azalea, and Josiah—and lockdown included some "bubbling" and therefore stronger bonding. As wider travel was canceled, it also included much more welcome time with my wife, Deborah; joint Scriptural Reasoning with Alexandra Wright and Steve Kepnes; long walks with our Shetland sheep dogs; and being delighted by the ways our core Cambridge communities of Lyn's House and St. Andrews Church, Cherry Hinton, responded faithfully and creatively to the pandemic.

We are grateful to series editors Kent Eilers and Kyle Strobel for giving us the opportunity to think deeply about a theme with such generativity as glorification. Writing this book together has been an amazingly energizing experience and during the bleakest moments of the pandemic often felt like a lifeline. Baker Academic has been consistently excellent throughout, and we are grateful especially to Dave Nelson, Bob Hosack, Anna English, and Tim West for steering us through the process with such care and patience. Ash has appreciated testing some of the ideas contained in this book in more formal academic settings, including the Systematic Theology Seminar at the University of Aberdeen, the Christian Theology Senior Seminar at the University of Cambridge, and the Practical Theology Seminar at the University of Roehampton. Other groups too, including the CMS Research Seminar in Oxford and the Bishop's Study Morning in the Diocese of Birmingham, have heard and enhanced the central ideas we discuss in this book. Ash is grateful to Roehampton colleagues and friends, including consecutive cohorts of always-energetic researchers undertaking the Professional Doctorate in Practical Theology; and to the "Science-Engaged Theology: New Visions in Theological Anthropology" project at the University of St. Andrews (funded by the John Templeton Foundation) for a fellowship and follow-on funding grant that has shaped chapter 4. Mark Scarlata provided some eleventh-hour transliteration assistance; Julie Gittoes joined us for one of our Zoom conversations to stimulate our thinking around the ecclesiology of glory we express in chapter 3; and Matthias Grebe has been a generous dialogue partner from the beginning. To these, and many others, we are grateful. We are also grateful to Baylor University Press for permission to quote the final poem, "Thomas," in Micheal O'Siadhail's *Testament*, and to Ellen Davis for permission to use and engage with her glorious translation of Psalm 145 as one of our doxological interlude texts.

Finally, Robbie Leigh has been an enriching source of ideas, insight, and deep friendship. He not only joined our text-centered Zoom conversations as a full contributor, but he has read and commented perceptively on successive drafts of each chapter, and when we were able to meet in person, he was with us. Robbie has been so closely involved in the production of this book that it is impossible to give him the credit he is owed in the pages that follow, but we can acknowledge from the start our deep gratitude for his involvement in this book and beyond.

Abbreviations

ANF	*Ante-Nicene Fathers*
CD	Karl Barth, *Church Dogmatics*
KJV	King James Version
LXX	Septuagint
NIV	New International Version
NLT	New Living Translation
NPNF²	*Nicene and Post-Nicene Fathers, Series 2*
NRSV	New Revised Standard Version
NRSVCE	New Revised Standard Version, Catholic Edition
RSV	Revised Standard Version
SC	Sources chrétiennes

Introduction

THE GLORIFICATION OF GOD is central to everything. As far as attempts go in the Christian tradition to imagine all things in relation to the glory of God, Thomas Traherne's *Commentaries of Heaven* is probably the most ambitious.[1] The work is prefaced with the aim of representing "Evry being, Created and Increated being Alphabeticaly . . . in the Light of Glory." In what would follow, Traherne had planned a lavishly rich, multivolume alphabetical study cataloging how everything (from A to Z) is created for glorification and destined for enjoyment. This remarkable project, which started sometime after 1670, is made more remarkable by the story of its discovery. The manuscript was found "smouldering on a rubbish tip just outside Liverpool in about 1967."[2] The idea of finding glory in the midst of ordinary life, and often in unusual places, is a central one in the theology of glorification expressed in this book. The alphabetical style of the *Commentaries* resonates with Psalm 145, also to be encountered later in this book as one of our doxological interlude texts, which likewise takes alphabetic shape. In both, the purpose is the same: to imply comprehensive praise and glory with nothing escaping the vivifying dynamics of God's glory.

While incomplete and cutting off well before reaching the planned "Glory" entry, the manuscript still runs to several hundred pages. Topics include objects (Armour), people (Aristotle, Adam), created things (Ants, Atoms), biblical themes (Ascension, Atonement), concepts (Abundance),

1. Traherne, *Commentaries of Heaven, Part 1*, and *Commentaries of Heaven, Part 2*.
2. Traherne, *Commentaries of Heaven, Part 1*, xi.

1

dispositions (Ambition, Attention), affections (Anger), and liturgical practices (Baptism), with many other themes included as subtopics. In every entry, at every turn, Traherne positions his topic in relation to glory. Ambition, for example, should desire glory, have its object in glory and so too its end, and effect glory in the world. What is significant is not only the encyclopedic range of the topics included and the way he shows how everything is attracted into what we are calling the "dynamics of glory," but also the interconnectedness of all things when attracted into glory and the way Traherne makes these interconnections gloriously attractive. There are cross-references throughout, "essential to the overall organisation of the *Commentaries*," with entries pointing to one another and leading beyond themselves, often to unwritten sections.[3] It makes reading the *Commentaries* linearly and speedily nearly impossible. Reading the *Commentaries* is formation, then, in the abundance of glory. It encourages taking time to see for ourselves the way Traherne sees the world: full of God's glory, on earth as in heaven (Isa. 6:3). Amazingly, the glory of God exceeds even the limitlessness of heaven, spilling out into the world, onto the street, into the materiality of the earth, and twinkling especially "in vulnerable life, in the lives of those who are considered the least."[4]

By the "dynamics of glory"—central to Traherne's encyclopedia project and the theology of glory articulated in this book—we mean the flow of glory that moves abundantly within God, radiates from God, and attracts everything into the fullness of God. No boundary is set around the scope of this radiantly attractive glory, this magnetic and inexhaustible reality. To be attracted into the dynamics of glory—that is to say, to be glorified—is to be formed into the fullest possible existence. As Irenaeus put it, "The glory of God is a human being fully alive."[5] That is what glorification means: being fully alive to God. And when you are fully alive to God, you are fully alive to others and fully alive to yourself. The Westminster Shorter and Longer Catechisms (1646, 1647) speak similarly of humanity finding their "chief end" in "glorifying and enjoying God forever." We want to push the dynamics of glory even further than this glorious

3. Traherne, *Commentaries of Heaven, Part 1*, xxvi.
4. Rivera, "Glory," 179.
5. Irenaeus, *Against Heresies* 4.20.7. Another rendering is "For the glory of God is a living man; and the life of man consists in beholding God" (*ANF* 1:490). For a profound theology centered on this concept, see Fout, *Fully Alive*.

vision to see glorification not only as the fitting end of the Christian life but also as its raison d'être—and not only for humanity but for all things. Like Traherne, we really mean that everything "Created and Increated" is called into the life of glory and to enjoy the fullness of that life together. God's ultimate, loving desire is "to gather up all things in him, things in heaven and things on earth" (Eph. 1:9–10). Even more, as Irenaeus says, the dynamics of glory make everything fully alive, bringing the fullness of God to all life as all things in their endless particularity are attracted into the radiance of God's glory.

The most inspiring challenge of thinking about glorification is thinking about the glory of God in relation to the full spectrum of created life. Every aspect of Christian theology, all dimensions of Christian worship and practice, everything related to social life, every level of church life, all academic disciplines, arts of every sort, cultures, politics, economics, every sphere of society, religious life, space, time, prayer, everything related to being human, and the overwhelmingly complex levels of reality beyond human comprehension—all this and everything else is brought fully to life by the glory of God. The cosmos is made fully alive, the church is made fully alive, Scripture is made fully alive, the Nicene Creed is made fully alive, you are made fully alive by the vivifying dynamics of God's glory! Glorification has, then, to do with God and the praise of God for the sake of God. And it has to do with the riches of a created reality endlessly transfigured by God's glorious love—and because of all this, glorification is unendingly interesting.

The Four Chapters and the "Ludes"

Everything in this book is examined in light of these dynamics. In this first chapter we set the dynamics of glory within the dogmatic context of the *regula fidei* (measure, rule, or essential core of faith) of Christian theology, the Nicene Creed. We explore how the doctrine of glorification is shaped by the trinitarian dynamics of the Nicene Creed, and how the Nicene Creed is shaped by the doxological dynamics of glory. We consider the single dynamic of glorification in three dimensions: finding glory in the divine life of God and in the world, giving glory to God, and receiving glory from God. In chapter 1 we also present our account of glory-centered reading, which we are calling "doxological reading." Some readers may

wish to start with this final part of chapter 1 and read on to the end of
the book before returning to our account of the Nicene Creed, which
is perhaps the most concentrated part of the book and may be better
understood in the light of chapters 2, 3, and 4.

In chapter 2, we discuss some of the seminal glory texts in Holy Scripture that together provide the biblical impetus for the dynamic we are
describing: the Psalms (as the summation of the main Hebrew Bible genres
of narrative, law, prophecy, lament, litany, and more), the Gospel of John
(as the maturation of the Synoptic tradition and much more), and the
Letter to the Ephesians (as the culmination of Pauline theology). Chapter 3, and its ecclesiology of the church "fully alive," explores the sort of
church life that comes to manifest the vivifying dynamics of glory. We
depict a vision of ecclesial life "fully alive together," seeking the glorious
unity that awaits the church as its chief end. We explore the fullness of
glory in terms of time and space, as well as offering practical examples
of the church's journeying toward the creedal mark of unity in the form
of Receptive Ecumenism and Pentecostal doxological practice. The final
chapter unpacks these dynamics in relation to Christian living by discussing how glory is experienced (as joy), embodied (in the smile), and enacted
(in Sabbath rest, blessing, and glorifying).

Before and after each chapter are the doxological "ludes." These are
contemplative interjections—creating time and space for doxology, for
glory. These invite you into the slow reading (on this, see again our account
of "doxological reading" in chap. 1) of the seminal glory texts discussed in
chapter 2: John 17, Ephesians 3:14–21, and Psalm 145. They might even
encourage you to slow right down into silence, into prayer itself. Perhaps
most importantly, the doxological reading of the sort we are recommending has intertextuality at its heart as the abundant meaning of individual
texts overflows, and each text is reread in the light of other texts. It is about
finding connections between "all things" in the continual reading and
rereading of texts, seeing nothing as standing on its own but everything
as dynamically integrated for the sake of God's glory. The deeper you
get into John 17, the deeper you get into Paul's theology, and the deeper
you get into the wisdom of the Psalms and the great doxologies of the
Hebrew Bible they contain. All this takes you deeper into the dynamics
of the Nicene Creed and, above all, into God. The doxological postlude,
finally, is Graham Sutherland's *Christ in Glory in the Tetramorph*—there

we face Jesus Christ, the Lord of glory, in whose face the glory of God is encountered.[6]

The Writing

As "it is hardly possible to speak of reading without thinking about the activity of writing at the same time," the counterpart of slow reading is slow writing.[7] The way this book has been written has tried to model something of the need to decelerate. Writing a book together, rather than alone, slows down the drive to quick completion. It has required time away from writing as the other reads drafts of chapters, inviting a particular sort of patience and stillness, and often leading to revision and rewriting. The thinking written up in this book flows out of spending time together in countless conversations over Zoom, structured around the doxological reading of the seminal glory texts featured in this book. This intensive engagement around rich texts has been generative again and again. Fresh ideas and images have occurred in that "space" between us and the texts. And these conversations also had the further dimension of a third partner, our friend Robbie Leigh. These conversations were a vivid, experienced sign and taste of the superabundance of glory and left us repeatedly feeling: How can we begin to do justice to this amazing reality in our writing?

Many other elements have helped shape this book. While working on *Glorification and the Life of Faith* together, we have also been involved in other writing that has fed into this project. For Ash, this has included two projects on spirituality.[8] Both flow from his doctoral work on Barth supervised by David in Cambridge, who also supervised Robbie's doctoral work on Barth.[9] True to the logic of glory, *Glorification* has "overflowed" into three further collaborative projects, now underway—on creeds, on the smile, and on joy.[10] David has above all been completing his twenty-year

---

6. See https://www.coventrycathedral.org.uk/visit/heritage/works-of-art/christ-in-glory-by-graham-sutherland.

7. Slee, *Fragments for Fractured Times*, 201.

8. Cocksworth and McDowell, *T&T Clark Handbook of Christian Prayer*; Cocksworth and McMaken, *Karl Barth*.

9. Ash's doctoral work is published as *Karl Barth on Prayer*; Robbie's as Leigh, *Freedom and Flourishing*.

10. The creeds project (funded by the Southlands Methodist Trust) develops aspects of chap. 1 in this book by exploring the experience of saying creeds among older Christians in

project of a theological commentary on the Gospel of John,[11] and following that through with other "overflow" writing.[12]

We have also been involved in one joint project. For over thirty years David was editor of *The Modern Theologians: An Introduction to Christian Theology since 1918*, through three editions. For the fourth edition Ash is the editor with Rachel Muers, and David is a consultant. *Glorification* is quite a short book, but the broad horizon within which it was written is best understood through the four editions of *The Modern Theologians*, and especially the fourth.[13]

For each of us, institutional and community commitments have been important during the time of writing. Important for Ash have been the University of Roehampton and his former institutional home, The Queen's Foundation in Birmingham—both places of ongoing inspiration.[14] The Parish of St. Lawrence Effingham with All Saints Little Bookham has been full of love and joy, especially so during the pandemic.

David has been "retired" and involved in a range of organizations and networks. Some have been of special significance for *Glorification*. St. Andrew's Church, Cherry Hinton, where his wife, Deborah, is a priest on the staff, has been a true home, a worshiping, doxological community, and during the pandemic its life was increasingly woven into its locality through a food bank and much else. His involvement with Cherry Hinton Primary School, as a governor with a special responsibility for the nursery and for English, has helped keep him in touch with the locality and the rising generation—and observing children beginning

---

the Roehampton area. The smile project (funded by the John Templeton Foundation through the "Science-Engaged Theology: New Visions in Theological Anthropology" grant at the University of St. Andrews) engages with developmental and social psychologists to construct a theology of the smile, and develops aspects of chap. 4 of this book. The joy project (funded by the British Academy/Leverhulme Small Research Grants) is called "Listening for Joy in an Age of Despair: The Religious Lives of Older Christians" and develops the theology of joy also explored in chap. 4.

11. Ford, *Gospel of John*.

12. Ford, "Ultimate Desire"; Ford, "Mature Ecumenism's Daring Future"; Ford, "Desire of Jesus"; Ford, the Costan Lectures, Virginia Theological Seminary (unpublished); and Ford, *The Wonder of Living* (forthcoming).

13. Muers and Cocksworth with Ford, *Ford's The Modern Theologians*.

14. During the writing of this book, Ash has edited with Rachel Starr and Stephen Burns a collection of essays in celebration of their Queen's colleague Nicola Slee: *From the Shores of Silence*.

to read and write has been a lesson in slowness. His participation in the Lyn's House community of friendship between people with and without learning disabilities has given another sort of transgenerational experience.[15] St. Andrews, the school, and Lyn's House have each gently but insistently raised the question as to where a community's priorities lie, and who are vital to its being "fully alive." The hungry? Children? Those with disabilities? Others who are rarely central to society's concerns? There has also been the Rose Castle Foundation,[16] focused mainly on forming reconcilers who work at peacebuilding across many types of conflict and division in several countries. One of its core formational practices is Scriptural Reasoning, in which participants from different faiths (in our case mostly Jews, Christians, and Muslims) intensively converse around passages from each of their scriptures on relevant themes. Such interfaith engagement has made an important contribution to the atmosphere in which our Christian theology has been thought and written. Scriptural Reasoning invites participants to go deeper into their own texts and traditions while going deeper into the texts and traditions of others and, through the understanding and relationships so formed, to engage more deeply and wisely with our world and its conflicts. At its heart, and vital to the integrity of each, is that, in different yet analogous ways for Jews, Christians, and Muslims, the study and discussion are done above all "for God's sake," for the glory of God, with other blessings flowing from that.[17]

Throughout our writing both of us have been involved in formation of various sorts—through university teaching, teaching and preaching in churches and at lay and clergy conferences, leading retreats, doing podcasts, mentoring, involvement with intentional communities, and more. All of this has strengthened our conviction of the importance, relevance, and even urgency of one of our desires in this book: to integrate doxology with the rest of theology, and with the whole of life, more and more deeply and thoroughly. For one of us the formative experience of this was in an earlier coauthoring. David's first teaching post was in the University of

---

15. See www.lynshouse.org and Ford, Ford, and Randall, *A Kind of Upside-Downness*.

16. See www.rosecastlefoundation.org, shortly to be renamed as the Rose Foundation for Reconciliation.

17. See Ochs, *Religion without Violence*; Higton and Muers, *The Text in Play*; Ford, *Christian Wisdom*, 273–303.

Birmingham, where he shared courses with his colleague Daniel (Dan) W. Hardy. Over several years they met regularly for one morning a week to do theology together. Slowly, through very wide-ranging discussion, the leading theme of a book emerged, as expressed in the three titles it has had in different editions.[18] That cross-generational collaboration has had a delightful resonance with ours, increased by the similar themes; and just as, after years of conversation together, David did the majority of writing in the coauthorship with Dan, Ash has done the major share of the actual writing in the present book.

Many more personal events have fed into the writing. At very different stages of life, we have each had the joy of welcoming new members of our families—Ash as a parent, David as a grandparent and father-in-law—sure signs of the abundance of God's glory. Alongside those born over the course of the writing of this book (for Ash, Lucy and Maisie; for David, Solomon, Azalea, and Josiah; for Robbie, George), we have also experienced deaths of loved ones (these include, for Ash, Edna and Julie; for David, Jack and June; and for Robbie, Mira). More public events have also shaped our book, especially the COVID-19 pandemic. We occasionally make explicit reference to it, but implicitly it is pervasive. It has been the most immediate, obvious, and global example of what can make glorifying God, and abundance of life, love, and joy, seem radically unreal, incredible, or inauthentic. We hope that our theology of glorification, centered on the God of Abraham, Isaac, Jacob, and Jesus, faces such challenges robustly and opens a way within, yet also through, their darkness, suffering, and death.

There remains one introductory issue: a definition of glorification. But we have decided not to attempt one. We offer a variety of images, metaphors, descriptions, evocations, concepts, ideas, creeds, narratives, and more. Our rationale is that we are trying to show what glorification is rather than to define it. We seek to invite readers into the sort of dynamics and abundant life to which we ourselves, together with many others down the centuries and around the world today, can in some measure testify. But that "measure" is never enough. All forms of expression fall short, in whatever artistic or other media. Where words are concerned, the least

18. Hardy and Ford, *Jubilate*; Hardy and Ford, *Praising and Knowing God*; Ford and Hardy, *Living in Praise*.

inadequate expression is probably not in a definition or in any other prose form, but in poetry and singing:

> Then I heard every creature in heaven and on earth and under the earth and in the sea, and all that is in them, singing,
>
>> "To the one seated on the throne and to the Lamb
>> be blessing and honor and glory and might
>> forever and ever!"
>
> And the four living creatures said, "Amen!" And the elders fell down and worshiped. (Rev. 5:13–14)

DOXOLOGICAL PRELUDE

The Nicene Creed

We **trust** [*pisteuomen*] in one God,
the Father, the Almighty,
maker of heaven and earth,
of all that is,
seen and unseen.

We **trust** [*pisteuomen*] in one Lord, Jesus Christ,
the only Son of God,
eternally begotten of the Father,
God from God, Light from Light,
true God from true God,
begotten, not made,
of one Being with the Father;
through him all things were made.
For us and for our salvation he came down from heaven,
was incarnate from the Holy Spirit and the Virgin Mary
and was made human.
For our sake he was crucified under Pontius Pilate;
he suffered death and was buried.
On the third day he rose again
in accordance with the Scriptures;
he ascended into heaven
and is seated at the right hand of the Father.
He will come again in **glory** [*doxēs*] to judge the living and the dead,
   and his kingdom will have no end.

We **trust** [*pisteuomen*] in the Holy Spirit,
the Lord, the giver of life,
who proceeds from the Father and the Son,
who **with** [*syn*] the Father and the Son is **worshiped and glorified**
    [*syndoxazomenon*],
who has spoken through the prophets.
We **trust** [*pisteuomen*] in one, holy, catholic, and apostolic Church.
We acknowledge one baptism for the forgiveness of sins.
We look for the resurrection of the dead,
and the life of the world to come.

Amen.

CHAPTER ONE

The Nicene Creed

TO GLORIFY GOD is to recognize and praise the scope of God's life, and to identify our lives in relation to God's glory and God's glorification of creation. When we stand to say the Nicene Creed, we are standing with the whole company of heaven to give glory to God, with Christ as our leader. We join the most honorable living creatures, the Seraphim, who stand in the presence of God, singing together to God: "Holy, holy, holy is the LORD of hosts; the whole earth is full of his glory" (Isa. 6:3).

In the first section of this chapter, we examine the way glory works in the words of the Nicene Creed and explore how the creed provides a formation in thinking theologically—and that means trinitarianally—about glory. From there we delve into the practice of glorification itself and explore the triple dynamic of finding, giving, and receiving glory. Then we turn to the relation between doxology and the idea of orthodoxy and how glory brings the practice of confessing creeds dynamically to life. We end this chapter with some reflections on the theological nature of reading, what we are calling "doxological reading," which has emerged as one of the core doxological practices in the writing of this book.

Glory, Glory, Glory

We have written this book for people seeking to be formed for the glorification of God by learning about God's glory. The Nicene Creed, along with other distillations of Christian wisdom, plays a critical role in the church's lifelong desire to learn more and more about the God we are called to glorify. The Nicene Creed, although short, is a massive affirmation of who the Christian tradition has come to think God "is." If learning is shaped around deep questions, and ones that need to be returned to again and again, the Nicene Creed asks the most searching question of all, "Who is God?"; and the response it gives to this most fundamental of questions is that God is Father, Son, and Spirit. There is nothing more significant to reality than confessing God as Trinity. Thinking creedally about glory, therefore, means thinking three ways about the singular intensity of the glory of God.[1]

Creeds are shaped by deep thought and shape further thought about God and all things in relation to God.[2] One may confess belief; but to confess a creed is really to *pray* a creed. When said or sung in the company of others and in the context and conditions of Christian worship, praise, and glory-giving, creeds are themselves doxological. Many of the words and phrases we say in the creeds are lifted from ancient liturgies.[3] The Father, the Almighty, the maker of all things visible and invisible; Light from Light, true God from true God; the Lord and giver of life—the origins of these words lie in the actual practice of Christians giving glory to God, first in baptismal liturgies, then all manner of ways, especially eucharistic liturgies. As well as the distinct literary borrowings from liturgical practice, the practice of building up glory, of piling affirmation on affirmation, is typical of doxology. This is more praise than proposition, more song than statement of belief. Creeds glorify glory, then, by performing what they instruct. They intensify the majesty of the one being affirmed, reflecting back the mystery of God's glorious being.

Moreover, the answer to the question of who God "is" is found in the practice of giving glory to God. So we pray in the *Gloria Patri*:

1. See Lash, *Believing Three Ways in One God*.
2. See Young, *The Making of the Creeds*.
3. For more on the way creedal adjectives correspond to some of the earliest eucharistic texts, see Williams, *Arius*.

> Glory be to the Father,
> and to the Son,
> and to the Holy Spirit,
> as it was in the beginning,
> is now, and ever shall be, world without end.

Glory is here dynamically directed to the three persons of the Trinity and across the three tenses. Like the Nicene Creed, the *Gloria Patri* is a formation against resting in the flatness of single ways of thinking about the glory of God by inspiring instead the richest possible multidimensional thinking. The glory of the Father cannot be seen apart from the glory of the Son and the Spirit, or the glory of the Son apart from the glory of the Father and the Spirit, or the glory of the Spirit apart from the glory of the Father and the Son. As you can tell, glorification gets more complex the more you think about it. It is no wonder that Hans Urs von Balthasar's magisterial theology of glory, published overall as *The Glory of the Lord*, fills some seven volumes. And by no means is the theology of glory best expressed in the form of multiple volumes of vast systematic theologies. It dwells also in the operant voices of hymns, songs, music, poetry, prayer, liturgy, icons, and spirituality, in the ordinary lives of people and communities, in the practices that make those individuals and communities fully alive, and much more still.[4]

Even the word *glory*, with its rich abundance of meaning, refuses single definition.[5] In Classical Greek, the word for glory (*doxa*) had to do with opinion and reputation and had many other meanings too, whereas the main Hebrew word (*kabod*) was associated with importance, honor, visible splendor, weight, God's revelatory presence in the world, and most importantly God's deity—divine majesty, holiness, beauty, and power. Glory has to do with God's gravitas and the "energetics of attraction" that calls everything into a share of God's life of glory.[6] These multiple

---

4. For two complementary accounts of the need to think expansively about the way theology is practiced in the life of the church, see Higton, *The Life of Christian Doctrine*, and Watkins, *Disclosing Church*.

5. For further reflection on the surprising lexical history of "glory" words, see Ramsey, *The Glory of God and the Transfiguration of Christ*, 23–28; Brunner, *The Christian Doctrine of God*, 285; Bauckham, *Gospel of Glory*, 44–46; and Barth, *CD* II/1, 641–43. In sociological discourse, *doxa* (glory) has taken on a life of its own—for example, Bourdieu, *The Logic of Practice*.

6. Hardy, *Wording a Radiance*, 48. See further Leigh, "The Energetics of Attraction."

meanings were gathered together by the writers of the New Testament and stretched further when the divine *kabod-doxa* came to be identified with the person of Jesus and the work of the Spirit, as we confess in the Nicene Creed.

In the Nicene Creed, "glory" words appear twice. The first appearance is when we say in the second article that Jesus Christ "will come again in glory [*doxēs*] to judge the living and the dead, and his kingdom will have no end." The future tense gives glory its eschatological orientation, its distinctive theological sense of forward propulsion into the ends of glorification. We can infer, however, from the "coming *again*" of the Nicene Creed that the writers of the creed assumed that the first coming, the incarnation, was the incarnation of God's glory in the world. The glory of God was incarnate of the Spirit and the Virgin Mary, taking flesh in the person of Jesus Christ for our salvation. Glory to the newborn King! The Son of God came in glory and will come again in more glory.

Following the biblical writers, the divine *kabod* encountered locally in the tabernacle is dramatically and daringly identified by the Nicene Creed with the person of Jesus Christ. Alongside the more technical terminology of *homoousios*, the writers of the Nicene Creed use "glory" language, then, to speak of the divinity of the Son. Glory means God. That Jesus Christ comes and will come again in glory is another way of saying that Jesus Christ is fully divine. Or, to switch this, the creedal identification of the Son as glory suggests that the Son of God is the primary way of speaking of God's glory. Creedally speaking, glory is not some abstract idea or fact or power but is identified in the concrete history of Jesus Christ. In the light of Christ, we are shown what the singular intensity of God's glory is.

When we say in the Nicene Creed that Jesus Christ, the light of the world, is "Light from Light," we are saying that he is glory from glory, God from God. Glory is the source of light, the light itself, and the radiating means through which glory enlightens everything. Light imagery indicates the closeness between the Father and the Son, and the enlightening presence of God beyond the Father-Son relation. This is the light that lights up the "theatre of glory,"[7] creating new intimacies between God and all things. This is the light that refracts from every surface so

---

7. Calvin, *Institutes of the Christian Religion* 1.4.8; 1.5.2; 1.14.20; 2.6.1.

that everything starts to radiate and so extend the glory of God. Indeed, insofar as the light of glory radiates, it attracts. As we said at the start of this book, glory is ever and energetically radiating, superabundantly filling the world with perpetual light, and attracting all things through Jesus Christ, "the radiance of God's glory" (Heb. 1:3 NIV), into its life-giving dynamics.

But that is not all. The Spirit too is glory. The second reference to glory in the Nicene Creed comes in the third article when we confess belief in "the Spirit,... who with the Father and the Son is worshiped and glorified [*syndoxazomenon*]." Intriguingly, when it comes to the Spirit, the creed moves beyond the heavily contested *homoousios* (in Latin, *consubstantialis*) language of the Father-Son relation to the peaceable language of doxology. Instead of saying the Spirit is consubstantial with the Father and the Son as the Son is consubstantial with the Father, the case for the Spirit's deity—and therefore divine equality with the Father and the Son—is defended on doxological grounds. The Spirit is not said to be *consubstantialis* with the Father and the Son, but *conglorificatur* with them. Gregory of Nazianzus, the co-convener of the ecumenical council at which the Nicene Creed as we tend to say it was devised, spells out the doxological argument for the Spirit's deity like this: "If He is to be worshipped, surely He is an Object of adoration, and if an Object of adoration He must be God."[8] If equal in glorification, the persons of the Trinity must be equal in divinity. Or, in full creedal idiom, Gregory says, "We believe in the Father, the Son and the Spirit, in their common substance and their common glory."[9] Of course, all the intimacy of mutual indwelling implied by the *homoousios* is assumed here too, but the meaning is enriched, intensified, and expanded through the glory reference.

When we say the word *glory* in the Nicene Creed, we are speaking therefore of the common substance of God, the Godness of God. The doxology reference in the pneumatology article safeguards the full divine "weight" of the Spirit just as the glory reference in the second article safeguards the full divine "substance" of the Son. And together, the references to glory in the creed safeguard the divine unity of God, a unity defined by

8. Gregory of Nazianzus, *On the Holy Spirit* (*NPNF*[2] 7:327).
9. Gregory of Nazianzus, *Oration* 42.16 (SC 384:84), cited in Brugarolas, "The Holy Spirit as the 'Glory' of Christ," 260.

mutually reciprocal relations. As Kathryn Tanner puts it, "Glorifying the one is therefore the equivalent of glorifying the other. To glorify the Son for what he accomplishes is to glorify the Father since the Son's own glory is from and of him; and the reverse, to glorify the Father for his goodness to us is to glorify the Son who carries it out."[10] So, as in the *Gloria Patri*, in the Nicene Creed glory is inseparably directed to the Father, Son, and Spirit in their full, glorious equality. Hence, in the christological controversies leading up to the creeds, Athanasius charged Arius with dividing up nothing less than the "one glory" of God common to the three persons when he denied the full divinity of the Son.[11] For Athanasius, the same (*homo*) substance (*ousia*) shared by the three persons of the Trinity is the divine *kabod*. One glory, three persons.

The two "glory" references in the Nicene Creed form theological claims concerning what makes God "God." These claims have long and controversial histories, but everything boils down to this: Thine be the glory! The great affirmation of the Nicene Creed is that God is to be glorified not for what God has done, is doing, or could in the future do for us, but simply for the sake of it. This is why rejoicing, as a form of praise, is so central to glorification. Praise "is response first of all to God for God's own sake, the response to God for 'who' and 'what' God intrinsically is."[12]

Of course, the doctrine of God remains unfinished when it speaks only of the glory of God in the life of God. God's glory is not so holy as to be insignificant for anything that is not God. As David H. Kelsey writes, "'Glory' is a relational concept. It denotes not just God's *gravitas*, but also the essential *self-expressiveness* of such gravitas, its resplendence or radiance or brilliance or beauty that attracts an 'other.'"[13] The God of glory desires to share the glory of God with creation. Think of how the main biblical words within the semantic field of glory (beauty, shining, radiance) have relational connotations; so too *doxa* and its close association with "concretely particular" places (holy ground), things (burning bushes and earthen vessels),[14] people (prophets), events (the transfigura-

---

10. Tanner, *Christ the Key*, 150–51.

11. Athanasius, *Four Discourses against the Arians* 1.6.18 (*NPNF²* 4:317).

12. Kelsey, *Human Anguish and God's Power*, 21.

13. Kelsey, *Human Anguish and God's Power*, 29.

14. For more on "vulnerable vessels and glorious treasure," see Culp, *Vulnerability and Glory*, 14–17.

tion, the crucifixion), and, ultimately, Jesus Christ—with whom, as later creeds would put it, we are consubstantially related.[15] These new intimacies between God and all things are made possible by the work of the Spirit. Indeed, you cannot talk well about glorification without talking about the work of the Spirit. For Eugene F. Rogers, the Spirit "models in the Trinity the glorification of God that it enables here below."[16] We can see now why it is proper that the Spirit is doxologically rather than consubstantially described in the Nicene Creed. The distinctive doxological work of the Spirit enables those saying the creed to become what the Trinity is: doxological by way of glorification. The pneumatology article in the Nicene Creed even indicates the practical means through which this life of glory is possible. We are formed from the dust to share in the divine life of glory by "worshiping and glorifying" the God of glory through the Lord of glory by the Spirit of glory. Saying the creed doxologically, in the context of praise and worship, gives concrete expression to our nature and destiny as glorifying beings.

As well as naming the dynamic unity of God, "glory" language designates the difference within the divine life of God. While the language classically used to distinguish the Son from the Father focuses on origins—the Son is not the Father because the Son is begotten *from* the Father, hence "God *from* God, Light *from* Light, true God *from* true God"—the dynamics of glory offer a different way of conceiving difference within the life of God.[17] Although the Son's giving and receiving of glory is inseparable from the Father's giving and receiving of glory, the Son's glorification remains particular to the Son, as does the Father's to the Father and the Spirit's to the Spirit. Each divine person gives and receives glory, and thus they work together in everything they do, but each gives and receives differently. Glory, while the same, is shaped differently by the particularity of the divine person giving and receiving it. It is because the Son gives glory to the Father that the Son is different from the Father, but not too different because that which is given and received remains substantively the same: glory. "Each returns to the others what it receives from the others; each

15. Kelsey, *Human Anguish and God's Power*, 30.

16. See Rogers, *After the Spirit*, 176.

17. These ideas—especially how "glory" discourse can lend itself to expressions of divine difference and divine relationality beyond relations of origin—have been significantly shaped by Linn Tonstad's chapter "The Lord of Glory" in *God and Difference*.

gives the other the same in a different way."[18] The persons of the Trinity are thus differentiated in the particularities of their giving and receiving rather than in their nature or in their origins.

Consider the Spirit article, which begins, "We believe in the Spirit, the Lord, the giver of life, who proceeds *from* the Father and the Son, who *with* [*syn*] the Father and the Son is worshiped and glorified [*syndoxazomenon*]." The question of where the Spirit proceeds *from* has attracted significant theological debate, climaxing in the *filioque* controversy and its long legacy of division and disagreement. In her exploration of the "Lord of Glory," Linn Tonstad argues that it is difficult to think of the language of procession apart from problematic relations of hierarchy, subordinationism, and contrastive power—a dynamic that runs counter to the overall creedal sense of the shared unity of trinitarian relations.[19] If the Spirit proceeds from the Father and the Son, then the Father and the Son, as the source from whom the Spirit originates, seem to get privileged above the somehow lesser deity of the Spirit. As others have noticed, such a hierarchy of procession is compounded by the ordering of the Nicene Creed and its allocating, at least chronologically, the Spirit as third to the apparent priority of the Father and the Son.[20] The Spirit is the last to be named as divine, and as such risks having the least to do in the economy of salvation. Cumulatively, and when read alone, an unqualified reliance on the processional "from," in the single (East) or double (West) rendition of the Spirit article, could run the risk of underdetermining the divine agency of the Spirit.

However, as we know, the Nicene Creed does not rely on derivative language alone to affirm the divinity of the Spirit. As the creed moves from the infamous "from" into the less famous doxological "with" ("who *with* [*syn*] the Father and the Son"), space opens to imagine the Spirit beyond relations of origins. The dynamic of shared but differentiated glory implied by the doxological "with" qualifies the processional "from" such that what the Spirit receives from the Father and the Son is the Spirit's by nature of what the Spirit already "is." The Spirit is already divine because the Spirit is already glorified "with," and therefore by, the Father and the Son in full trinitarian equality. In the doxological context of "with," trinitarian

18. Tonstad, *God and Difference*, 229.
19. Tonstad, *God and Difference*, 220–46.
20. Coakley, *God, Sexuality, and the Self*, 101.

relations are organized not around irreversible relations of origins but around mutual doxologies of gift circulating freely and equally within the life of God. When we say the Spirit "is worshiped and glorified," the Greek word is *syndoxazomenon*. Later, in chapter 3, we will recognize this word as a *syn-* word, as it carries the energetically rich prefix. Here, *syn* suggests something dynamic and circular (rather than linear and processional) whereby the Father and the Son with the Spirit give and receive the same, differentiated gift of glory. The language of doxology speaks of the dynamic back-and-forth, the sharing "with," the mutual enjoyment that comes from such an exchange, and the communion and communing that make the life of God fully alive. Redirecting theological attention onto the doxological "with" shifts trinitarian discourse from a focus on irreversible processions—who comes first and who proceeds from whom—to the imagery of reciprocity, of "side-by-side" relations, suggesting that whatever else we might mean by glory, we are dealing with something that is noncompetitively shared within the doxology of trinitarian relationality—and beyond.[21]

Beyond questions of origins, the key doxological question, then, is, Where does the Spirit proceed *to*? The work of the Spirit extends the vivifying "withness" shared between God beyond God, making it possible for all things to participate in, and be transformed by, the trinitarian movements of glory. When we glorify God by praising God for God's sake, we are attracted into this circular movement of free-flowing and fully freeing glory. Such attraction entails the transformation of everything. Dehumanizing relations of hierarchy and competition are changed into glorified relations of equality and communion. In Johannine terms, as will become apparent in the next chapter, the key imagery for this multi-dimensional "withness," which is used of Jesus, his Father, the Spirit, and those who trust and love them, is mutual indwelling in love. In the ongoing drama of glorification, we are drawn into patterns of mutual indwelling with God in the fullest possible community of love with God and each other. Glorification has practical consequences of the highest order: it is a radical summons to love.

Love is not mentioned in the Nicene Creed, yet insofar as the incarnation is the revelation of God's glory, the incarnation is the revelation of

---

21. Tonstad, *God and Difference*, 235.

God's love; and insofar as the Spirit is worshiped and glorified, the Spirit is lovingly worshiped and glorified as love.[22] The unfathomable intimacy the Son shares with the Father is the glory of mutual love, which is shared too in the loving intimacy of the Spirit, a unity in which the whole of creation is embraced. Love intensifies and enriches the attractiveness of glory. It makes glory even more beautiful. Glory and love are integrated most strikingly in the Gospel of John, as they are for Karl Barth in the central thesis of his doctrine of God: that the God of glory is the "One who loves in freedom" (*CD* II/1). That is what love, when it is most fully alive, does: it attracts everything into the freedom of a limitless community. Love is at the heart of the dynamics of glory, which makes the life of glorification a life of love. The greatest challenge of glorification is to respond to all things in love, because the lack of love—as well as distorted love, wounded love, failure in love, betrayal of love, rejected love, and refusal to love—is the chief indicator of life unfulfilled. Or, put positively, the dynamic of mutual indwelling in love is the most obvious mark of a life fully free, fully alive.

We have said there is meaning in what the Nicene Creed says about glory. There is meaning, as we have also said, in the prepositions associated with those references, not least in the way the doxological "with" signals the dynamic, expressive nature of glory. There is further meaning in what the Nicene Creed does *not* say about glory. While we can say that glorification has to do with God's Godness, which is identified in the specific, historical person of Jesus Christ and is shared with the Spirit, there is deep hesitation to speak with much fluency about what any of this really means—so much is left unsaid, unresolved, unexplained. The Nicene Creed offers, then, the pedagogy in a sort of trinitarian thinking that knows its limits.[23] Given its fundamental concern with the deepest things of God, the discourse of glory more quickly than usual hits the limit of what can be said and what can be known.

Many theologians follow the theocentric impulses of the Nicene Creed by grounding glorification in the doctrine of God. Balthasar, for example, organized his considerable theology of glory around the central idea of

---

22. Extensive engagement with love in relation to glory, and in deep dialogue with John's Gospel, can be found in Kelsey, *Human Anguish and God's Power*, 47–65.

23. See Karen Kilby's "apophatic trinitarianism" in *God, Evil and the Limits of Theology*, 31–44.

Herrlichkeit. The glory of the Lord "is precisely what constitutes the distinctive property of God, that which for all eternity distinguishes him from all that is not God; this is his 'wholly-otherness,' which he can communicate only in such a way that, even as it is communicated, it means his and only his."[24] Balthasar's most intensive engagement with glory begins suggestively in the dialectics of knowing and not knowing, seeing and not seeing, form and non-form—again, hinting at the way glory stretches language beyond the edge of words.

Barth goes even further in the mooring of glory to the deity of God. Barth's doctrine of the reality of God reaches its dramatic climax in his meditation on the divine perfection of glory. For Barth, as a divine perfection, glory is not something God "has," as if God could be God without being glorious. While an attribute speaks of something God "has in common with the beings of others," the language of perfection points "to the thing itself." Therefore, God's glorious perfection is something "He has . . . as His own exclusively. And not only so, but He *is* it."[25] In *CD* II/1, Barth examines the main perfections of God at length in pairs. First come the perfections of divine loving (grace and holiness, mercy and righteousness, patience and wisdom) and then the perfections of divine freedom (unity and omnipresence, constancy and omnipotence, and, climactically, the eternity and glory of God). Famously, Barth proceeds to designate glory the "sum of all divine perfection."[26] As the sum, glory is both the ultimate perfection of God (it is where his doctrine of God climactically culminates) and that which perfects the other perfections of God. Grace is perfected by glory; so too the divine perfections of holiness, mercy, righteousness, patience, wisdom, and so on. Each perfection is further perfected, integrated, and intensified by the dynamics of glory. There is a strange logic to glory, then, of "perfecting perfection" (on this, more later).

To speak wisely of the perfection of glory, we need "the light of the knowledge of the glory of God" (2 Cor. 4:6). Everything emanates from the dynamics of glory, including and especially truth, which shines forth in infinite excess. That we can know anything true of glory is itself a sign

24. Balthasar, *The Glory of the Lord*, 6:10.
25. Barth, *CD* II/1, 323. For a fuller treatment of Barth's theocentric doctrine of glory, see Fout, *Fully Alive*, 35–59 and 61–103.
26. Barth, *CD* II/1, 643.

of being attracted into the enlivening and enlightening presence of God's glory in the world. Put differently, the doxological "with" of the Nicene Creed qualifies everything that can be expressed theologically about God. Knowledge of God, the Nicene Creed teaches, begins not in the abstract but in the relational context of the story of salvation. By calling God "Father" we are already speaking as part of the glorious intimacy the Son shares with the Father. We are already "with" God as God is already "with" us. Although glory has a future-oriented eschatology that propels everything toward its shared end, the lived reality of glory in the Christian life shows that glorification is already enacted, already "with" us. Before we begin, we find ourselves on the inside of glory, already basking in the light of glory, already engulfed and changed by it, already identifying God from within. All this to say: there can be no contemplation of the mysteries of God's glory without already taking to prayer.

This book comes with the formational encouragement to integrate theology and doxology. In prayer, the theological fumbling around in the dark begins to acquire something of the sense needed to contemplate the strangest things of God. The deeper you get into prayer, the deeper you get into glory; and the deeper you get into glory, the more the imagination is stretched as it longs to do better justice to the deepening depths of glory experienced in the life of prayer. Even then, a theology immersed in prayer cannot purport to know more about God than is knowable. The always-elusive mystery of God's glory that loves in freedom continues to exceed even the grasp of the theologian "soaked in prayer."[27] Indeed, often the experience of prayer yields little clarity about anything. These sorts of doxological experiences, in which God is not "experienced" in any tangible sense, offer further formation in how much cannot be said about the glory of God. The experience of glory has more to do with "feeling" in the way Schleiermacher used that term, a sort of intuition of something that cannot be fully known. There is a "dazzling darkness" to the light of glory that overwhelms even exceeding brightness and the thickest darkness.[28] And yet, despite all this, these tensions and ambiguities do not diminish a theologian's passion to convey something of the hazy radiance of glory, however imprecisely.[29]

27. Evelyn Underhill, quoted in Wells and Coakley, *Praying for England*, 7.
28. Balthasar, *The Glory of the Lord*, 6:41.
29. Rivera, "Glory," 167.

Finding, Giving, and Receiving Glory

We have said that glorification has to do with the eternal movement of glory found within the life of God as the persons of the Trinity unite to share in the giving and receiving of glory. Further, glorification has to do with the movement from God to the world as glory abundantly radiates from the life of God to fill creation with the most resplendent light. Further still, glorification has to do with the movement from the world to God as everything in its particularity gets attracted into the self-glorification of God. The glory that flows eternally in God and makes God fully God overflows into the world and makes all things fully alive. As the effulgent abundance of glory flowing in the life of God overflows into the world, glory doubles back in doxologies of praise and thanksgiving. In this dynamic, glory glorifies glory.

Finding Glory

Before glory is given to God or received from God, it is found.[30] Glory is found in the divine life of God. And we are called by God, repeatedly, to live in the fullness of finding glory in the world. Glory is never not being found and refound in an ongoing historical dynamic of doxological discovery. The calling to a life of constant finding is a gift of the Spirit, but it is through the light of glory, the Son's radiating presence in the world, that what is already there is discovered. It takes glory to find the givens of glory in the world.

As the Nicene Creed implies, if God is the maker of heaven and earth, then every found thing, visible and invisible, is a sign of God's gift. The world is full of God's glory waiting to be found. Part of the strange logic of glory is that glory is found in the givens of the unexpected. Barth would say that because glory is a divine perfection, and known only in the perfection of God's knowledge, we cannot cling to a working knowledge of what we think glory is or where we think we might find it.

> All our preconceived representations and ideas of what from our own consciousness we think we are compelled to take for "God," have, when we

---

30. Our understanding of the "found" has been shaped significantly by Quash, *Found Theology*.

confess, "I believe in God," not indeed to disappear—for they cannot do that. . . . They have to receive from it not only a new content, but also a new form. They are not only improved and enriched, but they are turned upside down.[31]

Any thinking about glory cannot end more or less where it began. We are compelled instead to risk an encounter with the surprise of glory, the wonder of having everything endlessly turned upside down by a wildness that thoroughly exceeds expectation. We cannot get on top of glory to domesticate or control it. "God's intrinsic glory just is *what* it is to be God and the full richness of *who* God is."[32] This is why glory is always epiphanic: it is the wow moment, when the astonishing presence of God's divine glory breaks surprisingly into the everyday. Part of the surprise is that glory is found in unexpected places.

Moses encountered glory in the ordinariness of a bush. Others found glory in the everyday elements of cloud and fire. And Luther famously found glory in the cross. For Luther, the glory of God is not found in power, prestige, might, or strength but stretched out on the cross in the fragile body of Christ broken for us.[33] Liberation and postcolonial theologians have extended this central insight of Luther's by finding the glory of God "not . . . where normally expected, on the side of might, but among the weak—it shines in the midst of those who are excluded."[34] In a modification of the Irenaean dictum with which we began this book, Óscar Romero says, "The early Christians used to say *gloria Dei vivens homo*. We can make this concrete by saying *gloria Dei, vivens pauper*."[35] Accordingly, Cláudio Carvalhaes issues an urgent call in his liberation theology of glorification for Christians to head to the ends of the world to discover God's glory fully alive.

> Sometimes you will need to go to the mountaintop to see the glory of God. Sometimes and more often, it will be amidst your people that God

---

31. Barth, *Credo*, 12–13.

32. Kelsey, *Human Anguish and God's Power*, 29.

33. For a classic expression of Luther's theology of the cross, see Luther, *Heidelberg Disputation* (1518), 39–58. Calvin, similarly, puts the matter like this: "The glory of God shines, indeed, in all creatures on high and below, but never more brightly than in the cross." See Calvin, *Gospel according to St. John 11–21*, 68.

34. Rivera, "Glory," 175.

35. Colón-Emeric, "*Vivens Pauper*," 98.

will show God's glory to you. Every time you don't know where the glory of God is, go where the poor people are, and you will see Jesus, the glory of God shining in its full stretch. . . . For there, amidst the poor, the glory of God is in full swing![36]

Part of the call to glorification is the need to find and find again wiser ways of noticing the signs of God's glory shining brightly in forgotten or marginalized spaces—on the edges, at the ends of overlooked places. Being glorified means being receptive to new experiences of glory and responsive to new currents of thought emerging from such doxological encounters. As we shall see in the next section, part of what this means is being receptive to more than human doxology as revelatory of something of what it means for human creatures of God to praise God. The more glory is found over and over in the world, the more everything is attracted into the ceaseless movement of divine glory-giving and glory-receiving.

Giving Glory

How is glory given to God? Glory is given to God by all things in all manner of ways. Central to glory-giving is doxology: praise and thanksgiving, honor and adoration, singing and proclamation, petition and confession, baptism and Eucharist. Over the long haul, doxological practices such as these and many others shape actions, desires, and lives to such a profound extent that we come to "do everything for the glory of God" (1 Cor. 10:31). We become as Godlike as possible: *homo doxologicus.*

Even the weather glorifies God, as one of the great doxologies said in the Anglican tradition depicts. With its textual origins in the Apocrypha, the Benedicite would have been familiar in medieval piety as one of the canticles in the daily office, and it remains part of Morning Prayer in *The Book of Common Prayer.* It is worth reading (or even praying) the Benedicite slowly, aloud, and in its entirety to gain a sense of the fully cosmic scope of glory-giving.

> Glorify the Lord, all you works of the Lord,
>   praise him and highly exalt him for ever.

36. Carvalhaes, *What's Worship Got to Do with It?*, 238.

In the firmament of his power, glorify the Lord,
   praise him and highly exalt him for ever.

Glorify the Lord, you angels and all powers of the Lord,
   O heavens and all waters above the heavens.
Sun and moon and stars of the sky, glorify the Lord,
   praise him and highly exalt him for ever.

Glorify the Lord, every shower of rain and fall of dew,
   all winds and fire and heat.
Winter and summer, glorify the Lord,
   praise him and highly exalt him for ever.

Glorify the Lord, O chill and cold,
   drops of dew and flakes of snow.
Frost and cold, ice and sleet, glorify the Lord,
   praise him and highly exalt him for ever.

Glorify the Lord, O nights and days,
   O shining light and enfolding dark.
Storm clouds and thunderbolts, glorify the Lord,
   praise him and highly exalt him for ever.

Let the earth glorify the Lord,
   praise him and highly exalt him for ever.
Glorify the Lord, O mountains and hills,
and all that grows upon the earth,
   praise him and highly exalt him for ever.

Glorify the Lord, O springs of water, seas, and streams,
   O whales and all that move in the waters.
All birds of the air, glorify the Lord,
   praise him and highly exalt him for ever.

Glorify the Lord, O beasts of the wild,
   and all you flocks and herds.
O men and women everywhere, glorify the Lord,
   praise him and highly exalt him for ever.

Let the people of God glorify the Lord,
   praise him and highly exalt him for ever.
Glorify the Lord, O priests and servants of the Lord,
   praise him and highly exalt him for ever.

Glorify the Lord, O spirits and souls of the righteous,
    praise him and highly exalt him for ever.
You that are holy and humble of heart, glorify the Lord,
    praise him and highly exalt him for ever.

Let us glorify the Lord: Father, Son, and Holy Spirit;
    praise him and highly exalt him for ever.
In the firmament of his power, glorify the Lord,
    praise him and highly exalt him for ever.[37]

The Benedicite and its dynamic integration of earth and heaven prompt another expansion of the Irenaean dictum to include now the full cosmic scope of glory. The glory of God is the cosmos fully alive.[38] The angels, the heavens, the sun and moon and stars, every shower of rain, the seasons of winter and summer, the frost and cold, ice and sleet, storm clouds and thunderbolts, the land, the mountains and the hills, the springs and seas and streams, the fish of the water, the birds of the air, the beasts of the wild, the flocks and herds of the land—everything is caught up in the movement of glory-giving. Further still, glorification intensifies the particularity of all things, making each and every thing more fully alive to itself. All things are called to glorify God "simply by being themselves and fulfilling their God-given roles in God's creation."[39] If you have ever needed a reminder that there is not one way to glorify God, or that glory concerns the human sphere alone, or that other created things exist for anything other than the sake of glory, the Benedicite provides just such a formation.[40]

---

37. The version we are using is from the 1979 edition of *The Book of Common Prayer*, 88–90, which uses "glorify" as the leading imperative rather than "praise," as found in other versions. The Benedicite is sometimes known as "The Song of the Three" because Daniel places this prayer on the lips of Shadrach, Meshach, and Abednego (Dan. 3:51–90 NRSVCE). This passage, however, was eliminated from Protestant Bibles because it is not part of the Hebrew text of Daniel. For further theological engagement with the Benedicite, see Muers, "Creatures," and Higton, *Theology of Higher Education*, 163–64. For further doxological material in relation to creation, see Shakespeare, *The Earth Cries Glory*.

38. Deane-Drummond, *Eco-Theology*, 185.

39. Bauckham, "Joining Creation's Praise of God," 53.

40. Lynn White, who famously charged Christianity with a "historically dominant anthropocentrism," singles out the Benedicite as "the most remarkable" example of a "recessive gene" within Christianity that sustains "the notion of a spiritual democracy of all creatures." Despite its checkered textual history, he concludes that the "Benedicite may have more of a future than a past." See White, "Continuing the Conversation," 61–62.

The Benedicite places every creature in the cosmos ahead of the glory that human creatures give to God. Only in the final lines of the doxology are the people of God called to glorify God. The implication of such an ordering could be that humanity takes on a sort of priestly role, helping to gather and order and mediate the glory given by the rest of creation to God. But is that right? A better reading of the Benedicite sees the rocks and trees and the weather having, as it were, beaten us to it. When we give glory to God, we join "with" the glorification that has begun without us and before us and will go on after us. Our limited but vital obligation is to lend ourselves for a short time to the ongoing drama of God's unfolding glory. Indeed, there is a certain form of liberation that comes from being released from the anxiety of thinking we need to kick-start glorification: it has already started. We are called before anything else to enjoy listening to what is already happening in the extraordinarily rich doxological life of the cosmos fully alive.

If anything, human creatures are the ones in need of the priesthood of the rest of creation to glorify God as we ought. And if more than human creatures help us glorify God, the key question becomes, How do we repay the debt? Insofar as glorification is fully about God, glorification is fully about social and political and ecological transformation. The whole of creation is being formed together from glory to glory. As we are attracted deeper into the beauty of glory, we are drawn deeper into the world and participate more intensively and intentionally in the full scope of God's redeeming presence in the world. Part of the work of glorification, then, is about working against anything that blocks the flow of glory in creation and prevents created things from being fully alive.

As everything joins together in the glorification of God, the cosmos is made fully alive. Here, in a fully flourishing cosmos, all things overlap "with" one another as everything gets gathered in the same space without overcrowding, sharing without competition in the same end. The cosmos fully alive is a vision of an interconnected, weblike ecology of mutual interdependence, with intertwining and intensifying threads leading to the chief end of glorifying God. Glorification therefore entails the double intensification of the particularity and the mutuality of all things.

However glorification is given in the theater of glory, glory is given to God only as it is first given by God. The persons of the Trinity eternally give glory to each other, sharing with one another in the abundance of joy that is their nature, and give glory to others, calling all things into the glory that has been there since before the foundation of the world. Hence the (imperative) mood of the Benedicite and its calling of all things into doxological existence: "Glorify the Lord." When we respond to the imperative with doxologies of praise and thanksgiving by glorifying the Lord, we are not simply doing on earth what God is doing first in heaven. Instead, we partake in the same flow of glory that is already "there," already moving abundantly through and beyond God's glorious life of self-glorification. We are called by the God of glory into the glory of God. And we do all this through Jesus Christ, the "prototype of all doxology."[41] Jesus is not only the one in whom glory is perfectly found, or the one who perfectly gives glory, perfectly receives glory, perfectly embraces "both the *gloria* of God and the human glorification which it deserves and exacts," but Jesus Christ is himself *doxa*—"the very essence of glory."[42]

On this account, the glory we give to God over and over does not fill a need or lack in the divine life of God. God does not need to be glorified by the full magnitude of the created order to be complete any more than the fire in the burning bush needed fuel to remain alight. As Barth puts it, God in God's glory "is completely Himself and complete in Himself."[43] Since glory is given to God through the prototypical life of glory, nothing is added to God that is not already and eternally flowing gloriously in the divine life. This leads Barth to conclude that the glorification of God "is merely a confirmation of the divine self-declaration which takes place in and with the divine life-act."[44] The creature "echoes and reflects the glory of the Lord."[45] However, while the idea that glorification adds something

41. In *CD* IV/3, 48, Barth writes, "As the true Son of God, Himself God from eternity with the Father, He is the original and authentic image of the glory of God to the extent that in His life-act there takes place no more and no less than the divine self-demonstration in the time and space of the created world; to the extent that as the love of God seeking and finding man this act is human history; to the extent that His *doxa*, His power of revelation, is concrete event. But as true Son of Man He is also the normative original of the praise to be ascribed to God by man, the prototype of all doxology as the self-evident response to, and acknowledgment of, the self-demonstration which has come to man from God."

42. Barth, *CD* IV/3, 48; *CD* II/2, 140.

43. Barth, *CD* II/1, 667.

44. Barth, *CD* IV/3, 48.

45. Barth, *CD* II/1, 648. For a critique of Barth's logic of participation in respect of glory, see Fout, *Fully Alive*, 55–56.

to God might go too far, Barth's idea of "mere confirmation" does not seem to go far enough and risks making glorification, in some way, unnecessary.

It is never not necessary to glorify God. Indeed, it is *more* than strictly "necessary" or functional to glorify God.[46] Glory is given to God for more important reasons than getting something out of it or producing something new. Glory is given to God for its own sake, for nothing other than living into what is chiefly our end. For Jürgen Moltmann, glorification is best understood as a form of play, with "no purpose and no utility" beyond the meaning it derives from itself.[47] This gives the glory we give God— glory upon glory—a distinctive character, a beauty of its own. Another way of framing the relation between the glory given to God and the glory that already flows abundantly within the life of God is to see glorification, like praise, abiding by the "strange logic" of perfecting perfection and completing completion.[48] As we glorify glory, which is always "responsive participation" in glory's divine plenitude,[49] so we participate in the perfecting and completing of God's eternally perfect and complete glory for the sake of glory. The already perfect and complete nature of glory is further perfected and completed as the cosmos is made fully alive by the glory it gives to God. The glory we give to God, which returns the glory first given to us by God, intensifies what is, completely and perfectly, already found in the life of God.

Beyond finding glory in God and in the world, and especially in unexpected places, and then giving glory to God in all sorts of ways, there is even more to the abundance of glory: glorification entails the promise of being glorified by glory. Here "glory begets glory," to use Jason Fout's generative term.[50]

Receiving Glory

How is glory received from God? Receiving glory depends on the same christological dynamics as giving glory. As we give glory to God, so we

46. Jüngel, *God as the Mystery of the World*, 24–35.
47. Moltmann, *The Coming of God*, 323–34.
48. On the rich dynamic of "perfecting perfection," see Ford and Hardy, *Living in Praise*, 8–10.
49. See Greggs, "The Glory of God," 45–50.
50. Fout, *Fully Alive*, 6.

participate in the glorious flow of glory that is eternally and perfectly given in the divine life of God by the one who is consubstantial with the Father and consubstantial with us. Likewise, as we receive glory from God, so we participate in the Son's receiving of glory from the Father as the Father returns in perfect kind to the Son more glory. As the Son glorifies the Father, so the Son is glorified by the Father in a dynamic that moves beyond any simple contrast between activity and passivity: glory is given as it is received and received as it is given. In such a dynamic, the gift of glory—perfectly given and completely received in the life of God in simultaneity—is further perfected and completed.

When we glorify God, and so join with the Father's glorification of the Son, we glorify God with our bodies in the Spirit; and when we glorify God with our bodies, the Spirit glorifies our bodies. Here, the Spirit does not float free in some abstract spiritual realm but proceeds from God to rest on bodies, glorifying flesh, transfiguring materiality. Think of Moses's robustly full-bodied encounter with God's glory in one of the most celebrated biblical images of glory. As well as the "great sight" of the burning bush in Exodus 3 (v. 3), there is the smell of the bush that burns but is not consumed (v. 2); the touch of holy ground (v. 5); the hearing of the voice of God, who calls Moses by name (v. 4); the words Moses speaks with his mouth in response to God (v. 4); the anticipated tastes of milk and honey (v. 8); and the visceral feelings of fear and awe that made Moses hide his face (v. 6). The Septuagint captures this when it later says that Moses's body was "charged with glory" (Exod. 34:29 LXX). Moses knows God's glory because his body knows the glory of God. It has been charged and changed by it, even to such an extent that Michelangelo has Moses crowned with horns in his famous sculpture of the scene. The theology of glory is profoundly interested in materiality because at the heart of Christian theology, as summarized in the Nicene Creed, is the glory of God made flesh and blood in the person of Jesus Christ.

In her study of flesh and glory in John's Gospel, Dorothy Lee writes that "God in Christ has taken flesh, the whole world becomes replete with divine glory: everything now possesses the capacity to bear the beauty and splendour of God."[51] The divine *logos*, who dwells in glory, enters the world in flesh; and through the Spirit, the glorious intimacy shared between God

51. Lee, *Flesh and Glory*, 233.

is extended to all things. Importantly, the *sarx* of which John speaks in 1:14 suggests creatureliness in general rather than species-specific flesh: in line with the panoptic vision of the Benedicite, the glory of God in the flesh means the glorification of all flesh. As the enfleshed Word glorifies the Father and is glorified by the Father, so too the flesh of all living things is energized by the same magnetic charge of glory. As we glorify God with our bodies, so our bodies become resplendent with divine glory, transfigured to radiate the presence and power of glory in the world. We might not grow horns like Moses, but our bodies no less carry the marks of the glory of God, imaging glory in and through the course of everyday life. It is important that bodies are charged with God's glory in the everyday reality of Christian living, in and through the "fully fallible."[52] As Mayra Rivera writes, glory "appears not only as extraordinary phenomena, but more often as the transfiguration of the ordinary."[53]

In some descriptions of the Christian life, there is a tendency to move glory out of this world into the eschatological end of things. Often, "the final article in dogmatics, especially the dogmatics of Calvinist orthodoxy, has to do with the glorification of God."[54] In the "order of salvation" (*ordo salutis*) tradition, for example, the Christian life is said to reach its eschatological end in glorification. Having moved variously from election through justification, conversion, faith, and sanctification, the Christian life arrives at its final stage of glorification. When understood as a sequential itinerary, the *ordo salutis* runs into problems, however.[55] Such steady linearity and progression through discrete stages of the Christian life is an illusion that cannot match the unpredictability of the reality of life itself. As well as a theology of formation that can handle the unpredictable, nonlinear, and double-backing nature of lived experience, we are encouraging a theology of glory that sees glorification as a call into an ongoing dynamic: glory is here diffused profusely throughout every aspect of the Christian life. We are calling for the diffusion of glorification throughout the Christian life so that the deepening into the glory of God is both the grand finale in the story of salvation and the lived meaning of all things.

---

52. Tanner, *Christ the Key*, 274.
53. Rivera, "Glory," 169.
54. Moltmann, *The Coming of God*, 323.
55. For a careful tracing of the *ordo salutis* in the Reformed tradition, see Fesko, *Beyond Calvin*.

While the *ordo salutis* tradition might not work as a chronological description of salvation, it does work as a vivid articulation of glory's "even more" logic of abundance. What is more than being elected by God to be God's chosen people? Being called by name from before the foundation of the world. What is more than being justified by God? Being adopted into the life of God. Even more than being adopted into the life of God is being sanctified by God. And so on. The order of salvation articulates something of the sheer surprise that there is even more beyond the expected, intensifying what is already there with yet more new experiences of God's abundance. Calvin even somewhat hyperbolically suggests that the "glory of God . . . is in itself more excellent than the salvation of men and, as such, ought to receive from us a higher degree of esteem and regard."[56] Amazingly, being glorified is even more than salvation from sin and reconciliation to God. There is, as Barth says, a "super-abundance" to glory, which overflows as joy.[57] This logic of abundance means that there is always more to glory as we are changed from glory to more glory such that God's glory makes us not only alive but *fully* alive; so too glory makes us not only awake but *fully* awake (Luke 9:32). Even the meaning of *full*, as we will see in chapter 3, is transfigured from implying completeness or satisfaction to imagining ceaseless overflow that keeps filling without filling up. This sense of excess and ongoing unfolding of new forms of doxological life gets close to what it means to be made fully alive by the glory of God.

Doxology and Orthodoxy

Glorification entails change, formation, transfiguration, transformation. It is about being changed from glory to glory. Everything changes when attracted into the dynamics of glory, even the way we read the Nicene Creed. In the previous section we said that the doctrine of glorification is intensified by the Nicene Creed's theocentric impulses and its mooring of glory to the Godness of God. In this section we develop a suggestion made earlier in the chapter that the dynamics of glory intensify the Nicene Creed by making a doxology of the creed.

56. Calvin, *The Epistles of Paul*, 157.
57. Barth, *CD* II/1, 647.

One way of reading the Nicene Creed is to approach it as a guide for Christian belief. It summarizes and signposts the main principles of Christian orthodoxy: the God who creates, the salvific life of Jesus Christ, and the sanctifying presence of the Spirit in the world today. It functions as a framework around which knowledge, speech, and action can be articulated theologically. In particular, the Nicene Creed shapes thinking around the trinitarian dynamic of Father, Son, and Spirit and its refusal to rest in any one way of thinking about God.

When we say the word *orthodoxy*, we probably think first of "right belief" and the role the Nicene Creed plays in formulating and framing matters of belief. As we have said, in Classical Greek, *doxa* had to do with opinion, following the verb *dokeō* (to think, to suppose, to believe). *Orthodoxy* came to mean, in Christian usage, the standard against which Christian belief should be measured and the means through which the "utterance of a false faith that contradicts the glory of God" can be identified.[58] Within this sense of orthodoxy, I might read the Nicene Creed to fill in the gaps in my knowledge of God. When I want to understand better the claim that Jesus Christ is divine, I might turn to the Nicene Creed to learn how the persons of the Trinity fit together. I might then be able to speak more confidently about some of the technical terminology Christianity has used to describe these trinitarian relations. With a bit more digging, I might be clearer about the history of this terminology. I might be able to read between the lines of the Nicene Creed into the historical debates from which "Light from Light" and "begotten, not made" emerged and then proceed to make theological judgments of my own based on what I have learned.

However, for the New Testament writers the word *doxa* acquired another meaning alongside the classical sense of "belief." We recall that when the translators of the Hebrew Bible looked to translate the word *kabod*, they used the Greek word *doxa*. As a result, the idea of orthodoxy multiplies in meaning. It retains the classical sense of "belief" but acquires the "glory" associated with the Hebrew *kabod*. And with this intensified meaning of *doxa*, the meaning of orthodoxy gets stretched to integrate in the profoundest possible way belief in and worship of God. Stretching the notion of orthodoxy in this way brings the Nicene Creed fully to life.

---

58. Barth, *CD* III/4, 80.

Fully alive, the Nicene Creed is more formative than informative, more prayed than professed. And so the Nicene Creed ends, as doxologies end, appropriately with the word *amen*.[59] Ending with *amen* makes saying the Nicene Creed a glory practice in its own right; it makes a doxology of the creed.

The primary occasion for saying a creed is when people gather to do one of the most important things in their lives: to glorify God in proclamation, praise, and prayer. In the service of Holy Communion, as celebrated in the Anglican tradition, the Nicene Creed comes in the middle of the service—after the gathering, but before the breaking of the bread and the sending into the world to live and work to God's praise and glory. Being positioned in the middle of things says something important about the provisionality of the knowledge of things of God. It is to say, *These words of the creed are not the complete, finished articles but are offered to you, God, in penitence and in the hope that they will be redemptively remade by your grace and serve you in newness of life to the glory of your name.* Although "holy reason" cannot escape the gravitational dynamics of sin, neither is it held fully captive by them.[60] Knowledge of God is set free by the restorative work of the Spirit, who breathes life into everything, cleanses these words from within, and makes them fully alive by orienting knowledge for the sake of the glory of God.

When the Nicene Creed is read doxologically, its mood shifts, and the meaning of the Greek word that gets translated in English as "we believe" (*pisteuomen*) is brought fully to life. Rather than "believe," a more glory-centered, doxological translation of *pisteuomen* is "trust."[61] If we were speaking Hebrew, we would be using the word *emunah*, again with trust connotations and from which we get the word *amen*. Next time you say the Nicene Creed, try substituting "we believe" with "we trust" and notice the difference.

An epistemology of trust gives creeds a completely different meaning. Reciting the Nicene Creed as a doxology of trust is not about confidently reeling off a list of things I have come to believe about God, having reached an informed judgment based on the available evidence. There is nothing

---

59. On the significance of saying "amen" in creeds, see Lash, *Believing Three Ways in One God*, 1–3.

60. See Webster, *Holiness*.

61. Williams, *Tokens of Trust*, 6.

matter-of-fact about reciting a creed. Neither is saying the creed primarily about assenting to propositional content in some sort of a public declaration of doctrinal correctness. To say "we believe in God" can never be the same kind of statement of belief as professing belief in other things. Knowledge of things is real, but knowledge of God is more real: it is a gift of God worthy of glory. If anything, saying the Nicene Creed is an exercise in trusting how much I do not know and how much cannot be factually verified. When I say the Nicene Creed, I am affirming belief in matters, like glory, I precisely cannot get my head around, and yet I am called to believe in them anyway.

A good part of the Christian life has to do with believing things on trust. Since God is not an object to be comprehended, we trust in God to the extent that this trust glorifies us and all aspects of reality. I trust in those who devised the words of the creed, the doctrines they come to distill, and the scriptural wisdom they intensify. As creeds are often recited at baptisms, it could be said that the Christian life begins in these birth pangs of trust. I entrust my faith to the faith of others in an ongoing journey of discovery and especially with those who have learned to live the words of the creeds differently. I receive from others the things I did not know and new ways of knowing the things I already know. By saying the Nicene Creed, I am saying that I do not know alone, from one cleft in one rock, but as part of a greater community of knowing with multiple perspectives. The posture of prayer—and its dispositions of patience, attention, and receptivity—provides the right sort of conditions for these discoveries and surprises.

As well as relying on others to know the things I do not know, saying the Nicene Creed in the trust that comes from God involves entrusting others to hold faith for me, on my behalf, as I might at other times hold faith for them. This is why, in an Anglican service of Holy Communion, the Nicene Creed is immediately followed by intercessory prayers on behalf of the world, the community, and the church: to voice the irreducibly social character of knowledge. There may be times in my life when I cannot believe as I ought or glorify God as I should, and to say the creed during these times is to place my trust in those who stand in my place, holding faith for me as they might hold me in prayer. If there are aspects of these formulae that do not make sense or I cannot immediately fathom, if there are aspects that I find impenetrable or confusing, I go on saying them anyway. Despite my personal doubts, fears, and uncertainties, I go on trusting in God the Father, God the Son, God the Spirit. It is in relation to this reality that I understand myself: created and beloved and redeemed by God, and connected to a community of trust that is constantly expanding beyond boundaries.

Entrusting others with a matter as important as belief is a compelling, if risky, alternative to dominant narratives of mistrust that prevent us from being fully alive to ourselves and to others.[62] Understanding that the things I believe are implicated in the beliefs of others helps chart a way out of our socialization in particular kinds of rationality that assume I have to know everything for myself in order for anything to count. In an age when everything is verified and measured and evaluated to within an inch of its life, glory is beyond measure, given without measure. It speaks of the deep things of God that cannot be stacked up neatly. Indeed, as we said above, the Nicene Creed discourages precisely this type of thinking: the neat, the closed, the finished. As doxology, these creedal claims are deepened beyond epistemological certainty, beyond analytical grasp. By the canons of modern rationality, if it is risky business to entrust others with belief, it is an even greater risk to put trust in things that cannot easily be verified. Ultimately, then, reading the Nicene Creed as a doxology of trust is a formation in trusting and loving God. It signals the repeated desire to enter into the love, trust, and glory of God, and to live life fully from there, with all aspects of life affected.

In this section we have said that reading the Nicene Creed is brought more fully to life when read doxologically. Now, in the next and final section, we suggest that the habits cultivated by reading the Nicene Creed as doxological practice can be extended to energize other sorts of reading.

Doxological Reading

The traditions of Christian spirituality teach practices that seek to form people for the glory of God. Such doxologies include praise and thanksgiving, petition and lament, Eucharist and singing, social justice and hospitality, Bible study, fasting and feasting, and then all manner of everyday practices too particular to each of us to be mentioned here. These practices

62. See Ochs, "Morning Prayer as Redemptive Thinking."

become habits—not habits that need to be kicked, but habits to be in-habited. By inhabiting these practices and by seeing everything through them, we find that the glory of God comes to shape and structure our lives to such an overwhelming intensity that communities and individuals are themselves glorified. A core form of doxology in this book is the practice of reading. In this section we explore how reading itself, as a practice of formation, is intensified when caught up in the dynamics of glory.

As people of the book, Christians have always known the formative importance of reading Holy Scripture. A particularly rich theology of reading is associated with the figure of Mary, the one who bears God's glory in her body.[63] In iconography of the annunciation, you will often find Mary absorbed in the pages of a book—the book is likely the Bible or the medieval bestseller, the book of hours. In some iconography, the child Mary is being taught to read by her mother. In others, Mary is the one teaching her child, the Christ child, to read. The one who would be called "Teacher" (John 20:16) is first taught by his mother to read. Some early Christian writers went even further by speaking of Mary as a "book," our Lady of the Book, in whom we read of the glory of God indwelling the world. Mary read for the glory of God. What does it mean for us to read doxologically, without utility and for the sake of glory?

Reading doxologically means resisting the instrumentalization of read-ing in which reading is a means to an end, and that end is the acquisition of information. In his account of religious reading, Paul J. Griffiths names this sort of reading "consumerist reading."[64] This default mode of reading is about skimming, scanning, and scrolling through information in ever more effective and efficient ways. As the codex replaced the scroll, and the printed book the codex, and then the screen the book, we now "scroll" more than ever. But whereas the scroll, with its cumbersome choreography, once frustrated the need for speed, to scroll these days is synonymous with speed-reading, speeding through reels of words and data on the screen. To read has come to mean reading with speed.

The doxological reading inspired by Mary and recommended here (and developed further in chap. 2) is slow, gestative reading. Reading for glory

---

63. Our doxological account of reading is heavily informed by Nicola Slee's compelling reflections on reading in *Fragments for Fractured Times*, 197–204.

64. Griffiths, *Religious Reading*.

is less about extracting information from the page and more akin to the receptivity of contemplation: it is undertaken in and as prayer and for God's sake. In prayer, reading becomes *lectio divina*—it becomes holy.[65] Associated with the monastic practice of "divine reading" are the metaphors of munching and digesting.[66] This gastronomic imagery takes its biblical cue from the apocalyptic vision John received on Patmos in which he "takes and eats" the "little book" given by the angel (Rev. 10:1–11). There is something eucharistic about this language. What is taken and eaten is the life-giving Word of God. There is something also about Mary in this imagery. Reading is not about skimming or scanning. It is about the embodied act of receiving the Word of God through the words on the page. Mary has been taken to be the very literal embodiment of divine reading. She is the one who received the Word of God, nurturing the glory of God in herself—in her body. There could be few more direct ways of placing receptivity at the center of Christian living than reading.[67]

Reading the Nicene Creed provides a formation in reading for glory. As a part of the church's catechesis, creeds were memorized and internalized by those preparing for baptism and then recited, often by heart, before the congregation at their baptism. As Graham Ward explains,

> Committing the creed to memory was the means by which the Christian faith was to be internalized. It was not a matter simply of imparting knowledge, but participating in an ongoing understanding of the teachings of the faith through the practice of that faith—that is, enfolding one's experience of the world within the tenets of its teachings: being formed in and by Christ.[68]

Creeds are best read aloud, slowly, and in the company of others. They are to be said and resaid, read and reread. Whereas speed-reading is silent reading, voiced reading requires a different pace. Words on the page take time to say. The voice gets in the way of the rush to reach the end. Voiced reading requires attention to every word and to the voices of others as they speak these words. Reading as doxology involves humility and patience

---

65. *Lectio* has also influenced the practice of Scriptural Reasoning, which has informed our account of "doxological reading." See Buckley, "Rules for Scriptural Reasoning."

66. Leclercq, *The Love of Learning and the Desire for God.*

67. See Ford, *The Future of Christian Theology,* 173–75.

68. Ward, *How the Light Gets In,* 25.

and what we will later call, following Bonhoeffer, the "stillness" of time. Reading takes time and is best undertaken in a community of mutual readers reading in a spirit of generosity and openness to diverse interpretations of the same text. Above all, the specifically doxological nature of reading lies in its being undertaken before God and for the sake of God.

We are encouraging a "slow" reading of this book, like *lectio*. To this contemplative end, the doxological interludes marking the edges of the chapters act as "speed bumps." These are interruptions for glory, calling attention to the significance of the edges of things as well as to prayer itself. They are intended to disrupt the rapidity of reading and to resist the consumption of information by "wasting time" in the playfulness of reading.[69] This is our way of allowing the pages of this book to perform in practice the movement between reading and praying we are recommending in theory.

We are also inviting you to consider reading the chapters between these doxological interruptions as contemplative exercises. With Mary as our guide, we are inviting you to allow what is being read to be absorbed by the body, into your body. We are inviting you to chew this book in small morsels. It is not a book written to be scrolled through or skimmed over. Instead, the doxological reading we have in mind is more like Sabbath reading. "Reading brings the soul to rest," to Sabbath rest—a theme we will return to at the end of this book.[70] Rest with these words, and in so doing rest in the Word, the one who came in glory, and took flesh in Mary's glorified body, and will come again in glory to judge the quick and the dead.

To conclude, we have said glorification encompasses the glory given and received in the divine life of God by each of the divine persons of God. It also encompasses the glory radiating from God that lights up the world, the glory given to God by all things in doxologies of praise and thanksgiving, and the glory all things receive from God when attracted into the life and light of glory. These different movements of glory cohere as a single, inseparable dynamic. Glory circulates within the divine life of God in mutually intensifying exchanges of giving and receiving glory. As glory circulates, the dynamic expands in ever-intensifying waves of glory,

---

69. For a discussion of prayer as "time wasting," see McCabe, *God Matters*, 215–25.
70. Illich, *In the Vineyard of the Text*, 63.

stretching through time, reaching out indefinitely, pulling all things into its orbit, and creating a dynamic flow of glory in the world.

So far we have dwelt largely in the imperative mood of the Benedicite (with its great summoning of all things into the glorification of God) and the indicative mood of the Nicene Creed (with its string of affirmations of who God is). We end with a move into the other moods of faith.[71] The dynamics of glory gather up the moods of faith, weaving them together in such a way that makes them fully alive, fully integrated and intensified and balanced.

There is the subjunctive mood of exploration and experimentation. This is the mood of "may be" and "might be," in which different possibilities are imagined and conceived. What sort of world is possible when made fully alive by the glory of God? We have said that taking the Nicene Creed seriously means being fully alive to the glory of God that is inexhaustibly surprising, found in unexpected places and spaces. The mood of surprise is taken up again in the ecclesiology of glory explored in chapter 3 when we will embrace the possibility of the church moving toward the known unknown future of unity, holiness, catholicity, and apostolicity as signs of the church being made fully alive by God's glory. Then there is the optative, which is the mood of desire, desiring, and being desired. The theme of desire is fundamental to glory. God's ultimate desire is for all things to be attracted into the desire of God, for everything to be shaped in line with it, and to desire what God desires: union, mutual indwelling, love, joy. What does it mean to desire Christ's "coming again" in glory? How can desires be shaped, primed, and energized toward ever-wiser ways of finding, giving, and receiving glory? What does it mean to desire more of the glory of God as Moses desired to see more of God's glory? Important here is not only the description of desire but also its discernment and transfiguration. Indeed, there is a rich Christian tradition of understanding worship as the main crucible through which Christians are formed to desire what we most truly should desire.

Finally, there is the interrogative mood. The theme of glory raises a host of critical questions that encourage ongoing testing, critique, interrogation, and lament. What happens when the glorification of God goes wrong and gets malformed by the distorting dynamics of sin? How do we

---

71. For more on the "moods of faith," see Ford, *Christian Wisdom*, 45–51.

resist glorification becoming further conscripted into the corrupt logic of "God, gold, and glory"? "How can we celebrate wonder when even a cursory look at history reveals that systems of injustices expose the lives of some people to indescribable suffering, when claims to glory have so often been part of the very justification of unjust systems?"[72] There can be no doubt that glory can be, and has been, used to this end. While the Nicene Creed is more indicative than interrogative, there is still a realism about what sin can do. The Nicene Creed does not tell the story of a completely rosy world. By recalling the crucifixion, suffering, and death of the Son of God, the Nicene Creed is alert to the human condition's propensity to fall short of the glory of God. The dynamics of glory, however attractive, however beautiful, are met with violent resistance as the one who comes in glory is put to death on the cross. A theology of glory that takes the Nicene Creed seriously is profoundly interested in the stated indicatives of the creed, as well as the gaps between them and the questions they raise. What are the idols that lurk in our desires and misdirect our doxologies? What blocks the dynamics of glory and gets in the way of "Evry being," as Traherne has it, feeling fully alive? Saying the Nicene Creed week in, week out means that these questions are never not being asked and re-asked. Any seeker of glory formed by the creed should be ceaselessly and passionately attentive to these questions. Yet what comes from the Nicene Creed is a tipping of the balance. Sin, doubt, and suspicion do not claim the last words. As we come to place our love in the one who will come again in glory, we come to trust the massive affirmation of the Christian faith that the last word is the glorification and enjoyment of God forever.

72. Rivera, "Glory," 168.

DOXOLOGICAL INTERLUDE

John 17

After Jesus had spoken these words, he looked up to heaven and said, "Father, the hour has come; **glorify** [*doxason*] your Son so that the Son may **glorify** [*doxasē*] you, since you have given him authority over all people [*pasēs sarkos*], to give eternal life to all whom you have given him. And this is eternal life, that they may know you, the only [*monon*] true God, and Jesus Christ whom you have sent. I **glorified** [*edoxasa*] you on earth by finishing the work [*to ergon teleiōsas*] that you gave me to do [*poiēsō*]. So now, Father, **glorify** [*doxason*] me in your own presence with **the glory** [*tē doxē*] that I had in your presence before the world existed [*pro tou ton kosmon einai*].

I have made **your name** [*sou to onoma*] known to those whom you gave me from the world. They were yours, and you gave them to me, and they have kept your word [*ton logon sou*]. Now they know that everything you have given me is from you; for the words that you gave to me I have given to them, and they have received them and know in truth that I came from you; and they have believed that you sent me. I am asking on their behalf; I am not asking on behalf of the world, but on behalf of those whom you gave me, because they are yours. All mine are yours, and yours are mine; and I have been **glorified** [*dedoxasmai*] in them. And now I am no longer in the world, but they are in the world, and I am coming to you. **Holy Father** [*pater hagie*], protect them **in your name** [*en tō onomati sou*] that you have given me, so that they may be one, as we are one. While I was with them, I protected them in your name that you have given me. I guarded them, and not one of them was lost except the one destined to be lost, so that the scripture might be fulfilled. But now I am coming to you, and I speak these things in the world so that they may have **my joy made complete** [*tēn charan tēn emēn peplērōmenēn*] in themselves.

I have given them your word, and the world has hated them because they do not belong to the world, just as I do not belong to the world. I am not asking you to take them out of the world, but I ask you to protect them from the evil one. They do not belong to the world, just as I do not belong to the world. **Sanctify** [*hagiason*] them in the truth; your word [*logos*] is truth. As you have sent me into the world, so I have sent them into the world. And for their sakes **I sanctify** [*hagiazō*] myself, so that they also may be **sanctified** [*hēgiasmenoi*] in truth.

I ask not only on behalf of these, but also on behalf of those who will believe in me through their word [*logou autōn*], that they may all be one. As you, Father, are in me and I am in you, may they also be in us, so that the world may believe that you have sent me. **The glory** [*tēn doxan*] that you have given me I have given them, so that they may be one, as we are one, I in them and you in me, that they may become **completely one** [*teteleiōmenoi eis hen*], so that the world may know that you have sent me and have **loved** [*ēgapēsas*] them even as you have **loved** [*ēgapēsas*] me. Father, **I desire** [*thelō*] that those also, whom you have given me, may be with me where **I am** [*eimi egō*], to see **my glory** [*tēn doxan tēn emēn*], which you have given me because you **loved** [*ēgapēsas*] me before the foundation of the world [*pro katabolēs kosmou*].

Righteous Father, the world does not know you, but I know you; and these know that you have sent me. I made **your name** [*to onoma sou*] known to them, and I will make it known, so that **the love** [*hē agapē*] with which you have **loved** [*ēgapēsas*] me may be in them, and I in them.

CHAPTER TWO

Scripture

THE BIBLE CAN BE READ in the light of the glory of God and for the sake of the glory of God. Learning to read like this is at the heart of our Christian theology of God's glory, and this chapter, following on from the initial description of doxological reading in the previous chapter, shares what we have learned. It is a practice of engaging simultaneously with the text, with the God to whom it testifies, with the community of other readers, and with the world God has created, sustains, and loves, all in relation to glory.

We are not trying to give a full account of what the Bible says about the glory of God and glorifying God—that would take many large books. We are concentrating on three seminal texts.

First is John as a Gospel of glory. It teaches us how to read doxologically in the presence of Jesus and in a way that is centered on who he is. It has what we call a "deep plain sense": words, phrases, imagery, teachings, conversations, characters, and stories that can make sense at first reading but also invite readers into repeated, slow rereading in order to go deeper and deeper. Part of this is due to the careful crafting of the Gospel so that the meaning of the earlier parts is enriched by the later parts, encouraging further rereading. As if the text of John itself is not enough, its meaning is further and inexhaustibly enhanced by its intertextuality—how it relates to other texts though an interplay that takes us deeper into both John and the others. These include John's own Bible (especially the Septuagint, the translation of Israel's Scriptures from Hebrew into Greek), the Gospels of Matthew, Mark, and Luke (the Synoptic Gospels—we especially explore the fascinating relationship between John and their key "glory event" of the transfiguration), and the letters ascribed to Paul. All this follows our interlude text, the profound doxology in the prayer of Jesus in John 17, where we have directed readers toward some of its most fruitful intertexts.

John's own doxological writing has helped inspire ours. So too has the next text, the Letter to the Ephesians.[1] Our second interlude passage, Ephesians 3:14–21, following this chapter, is a prayer of superabundant glory and love. We explore its riches further in relation to the rest of the letter, whose ecology of praise, blessing, and wisdom embraces the whole of creation—past, present, and future. Its multidimensional theology of God, the crucified and resurrected Jesus Christ, the Holy Spirit, and the church is interwoven with the ordinary life of a Christian community, including its problems and suffering. It is a life marked by doxological desire and practice: overflowing speech in *parrhēsia*, and the singing of psalms, hymns, and spiritual songs.

The singing includes our third interlude text, Psalm 145, which follows chapter 3 below. It is perhaps the archetypal psalm of praising, blessing, and glorifying God for God's sake. We have been especially inspired by the translation and interpretation of it by Ellen Davis and by the 150 new psalms by Micheal O'Siadhail that she commends, and O'Siadhail also provides the conclusion to our closing reflection on greatness, love, and trust in Psalm 145 and the Gospel of John.

Reading John, Gospel of Glory[2]

"And the Word became flesh and lived among us, and we have seen his glory, the glory as of a father's only son, full of grace and truth" (John 1:14). That has been one of the most important verses in the history of Christian theology, and it speaks of glory twice. The Word has already been identified with God (1:1); now the Word is identified with a particu-

---

1. Scholars differ about whether or not Ephesians is by Paul. For us what is most important is that this letter comes from within the mature Pauline tradition and can be read as a culminating expression of theology in line with Paul. See Ford, *Self and Salvation*, 107–36.

2. Bauckham, *Gospel of Glory*.

lar person, Jesus Christ. So his glory is both the glory of God and glory embodied in a human being. This is glory on earth as in heaven.

The rest of the Gospel of John tells the story of this person, this glory. Whereas the other Gospels testify to the visible glory of Jesus in specific events, above all in his transfiguration (see further below), John's whole Gospel is pervaded by glory.[3] John's sense of the supra-pervasiveness of glory has inspired our dynamic expansion of the *ordo salutis* tradition that sees glorification diffused throughout the Christian life. After its central position in the Prologue, glory frames chapters 2–12 (often called "The Book of Signs"). The account of the first sign, turning water into wine at a wedding in Cana, concludes, "Jesus did this, the first of his signs, in Cana of Galilee, and revealed his glory" (2:11). This suggests that we are to read all the other signs he does as likewise revealing his glory, and the account of the culminating one, the raising of Lazarus from death, is explicit about this: "Did I not tell you that if you believed, you would see the glory of God?" (11:40; cf. 11:4). The Book of Signs concludes with chapter 12, where Jesus, whose "soul is troubled" as he faces his death, prays, "Father, glorify your name" (12:28). This intensifies the characteristic Johannine transformation of the meaning of glory by connecting it with the death of Jesus.

Then come the Farewell Discourses (John 13–17), the most important body of teaching in this Gospel. This too is framed by glory (see especially 13:31–32 and 17:1–5, 22–24). The prayer in John 17 opens up the heights, depths, and breadth of glory. There, in the climactic "hour" of his life, as he heads for death, Jesus not only reveals the heart of his relationship of mutual glorification with his Father—"Father, the hour has come; glorify your Son so that the Son may glorify you"—and roots this "hour" in "the glory that I had in your presence before the world existed" (17:1–5). He also opens up that relationship—which the rest of the prayer shows to be one of glorifying that is inseparable from eternal life, trust, joy, holiness, truth, and, above all, love—to those who trust and love him: "The glory that you have given me I have given them" (17:22).

---

3. For a fuller account of glory in the Gospel of John, see Ford, "'To See My Glory.'" For an even fuller account in the form of commentary on the whole Gospel, see Ford, *Gospel of John*. For an account of the approach to understanding the Bible followed in that commentary and in the present volume, combining scholarship, hermeneutics, and theology, see Ford, *Christian Wisdom*, 52–89.

We will return to that most profound chapter, but now jump to the endings of the Gospel in chapters 20 and 21 to reflect on their striking implications for the significance of seeing and of reading.[4] John 20 is full of seeing (vv. 1, 5, 6, 8, 12, 14, 18, 20, 25, 27, 29). Seeing the risen Jesus is clearly very important, and the testimony being given is part of what 1:14 means by "we have seen his glory." But 20:29 springs a surprise. Thomas has just given the ultimate acknowledgment of who Jesus is: "My Lord and my God!" (20:28). But then Jesus says to him, "Have you believed because you have seen me? Blessed are those who have not seen and yet have come to believe" (20:29).

Then John immediately moves into a key statement about his own writing in relation to coming to believe. "Now Jesus did many other signs in the presence of his disciples, which are not written in this book. But these are written so that you may come to believe that Jesus is the Messiah, the Son of God, and that through believing you may have life in his name" (20:30–31). In other words, reading this text is a way to come to meet, believe, and trust in Jesus, and to have ongoing *life* in this relationship with him. Those "who have not seen and yet have come to believe" by reading this Gospel are "blessed." They cannot say, in the same way as Thomas and other original eyewitnesses can, that "we have seen his glory," but they can read the testimony to this glory right through the Gospel, can meet Jesus through reading, and can go on living in his name. The gift of glory by Jesus ("The glory that you have given me I have given them") is given through reading and trusting this Gospel. This is doxological reading, reading ourselves into the most amazing, encompassing, and pervasive reality conceivable, the glory of God.

But that is not all. John 21 vividly illustrates the transition from seeing to reading that is crucial to the ongoing life of the church. There is one further resurrection appearance of Jesus, but this time there is no straightforward seeing. It opens, "After these things Jesus showed himself again to the disciples by the Sea of Tiberias; and he showed himself in this way" (21:1). The word for "showed" can mean "revealed," not necessarily by sight, and in this way clearly places an emphasis on the mode of appearance. So how does Jesus reveal himself in this chapter?

He stands on the beach, but "the disciples did not know that it was Jesus" (John 21:4). He is not straightforwardly recognizable, and John

4. For more on these chapters, see Ford, *Gospel of John*, 394–432.

does not say why. They have a conversation with him, he directs where to cast their nets, leading to a large catch of fish, and then "that disciple whom Jesus loved said to Peter, 'It is the Lord!'" The realization seems to have come by recognizing a beloved voice. "When Simon Peter heard that it was the Lord, he ... jumped into the sea" (21:7). Peter trusts the testimony he has heard and goes to Jesus. Even when they are all on the shore and invited by Jesus to have breakfast, the mystery of recognizability continues: "Now none of the disciples dared to ask him, 'Who are you?' because they knew [note: *knew*, not *saw*] it was the Lord. Jesus came and took the bread and gave it to them" (21:12–13). It seems as if John is suggesting some basic ways in which those who join the church will meet Jesus—through his words; through testimony to who he is, given by those who love him; and through his mysterious presence while followers gather together for meals. In later terms: through word and sacrament.

But there is yet more in this chapter. Peter, who had denied Jesus three times during his trial, is gently restored by Jesus, who asks him three times, "Do you love me?" He is entrusted with responsibility for the community—"Feed my lambs. ... Feed my sheep"—and he is told the cost of following Jesus. This is the final explicit mention of glory in this Gospel: Jesus "said this to indicate the kind of death by which he [Peter] would glorify God" (John 21:15–19). Readers are left in no doubt, as the emergent church was soon to learn from experience, that following Jesus can involve not only being utterly and gently loved and forgiven, together with being called into lifelong responsibility, but also going the way of the cross to the point of glorifying God by dying. Reading ourselves into glory through the Gospel can lead there.

Yet even that is not the end. Peter asks about the future of "the disciple whom Jesus loved" and is told, "If it is my will that he should remain until I come, what is that to you? Follow me!" (John 21:22). Other Gospels have vivid apocalyptic pictures of a future in which "they will see 'the Son of Man coming in clouds' with great power and glory" (Mark 13:26//Matt. 24:30//Luke 21:27). John does not deny that but focuses on who is at the heart of it, Jesus—"*until I come.*" The future is Jesus, the "I" that is so central for John, especially in the "I am" sayings of Jesus, identifying him with the presence of God. This future of course means seeing his glory, which is revealed through his life, death, resurrection, and breathing the Spirit into his followers. Jesus is on both sides of death, on both sides of whatever the future holds. One can be (and perhaps ought to be) agnostic about many other things, but his presence, whether visible or invisible, can be trusted, both now and in the future. This Gospel strongly affirms the "not yet" life beyond death but does it almost in an "of course" way. "In my Father's house there are many dwelling places. If it were not so, would I have told you that I go to prepare a place for you? And if I go and prepare a place for you, I will come again and will take you to myself, so that where I am, there you may be also" (John 14:2–3). This "not yet" is united with the "already" of now by that "I am" of Jesus, as he goes on to tell Thomas, "I am the way, and the truth, and the life" (14:6).[5] This living person, embodying the truth of God and God's creation, is the trustworthy connection, the way, between the present and the future. This relativizes speculation about the future and relativizes even death itself. The one essential, as Jesus says to his anxious disciples, is "Do not let your hearts be troubled. Believe in God, believe also in me" (14:1). In the final conversation of Jesus with Peter, this translates into the imperative invitation "Follow me!" And whether one's future is to give one's life in following Jesus or to "remain until I come," both can be about glorifying God.

That word *remain* leads into what really is the end of this Gospel. The Greek verb is *menō*, a very important word in John, meaning also "to abide, rest on, dwell in, live in, stay, last, continue, endure, or await"; and the noun from it, *monē*, gives "dwelling places" in 14:2. During his crucifixion Jesus had created a new family-and-beyond-family household of his mother and the disciple he loved (19:26–27), so that is where we are to imagine the beloved disciple continuing to live. It is, as it were, the "hidden" church, brought into being directly by the crucified Jesus, and its two known members are anonymous in this Gospel. There is a more public church too, with Peter, a named leader, heading for the drama of martyrdom.

What goes on in the hidden church is now described. "This is the disciple who is testifying to these things and has written them, and we know that his testimony is true" (John 21:24). This is writing based on eyewitness knowledge, and the "we know" involves a community too. But what is behind the writing? It has all the marks of much prayer and

5. For much more on this fascinating and important chapter, see Ford, *Gospel of John*, 269–88.

meditation, much reading (the style is especially full of echoes of the Septuagint, beginning with the opening words of Genesis in John 1:1), and the experience of the early decades of living and worshiping in the young Christian church. The author knows of many other accounts of Jesus, whether oral or written (20:30; 21:25), and has distilled what he has come to discern as their essence. John (we use the traditional name for the author, but it is not in the text) includes far fewer incidents than the Synoptic Gospels but writes at greater length and goes deeper into the ones that are selected.[6] And he writes (in line with his own testimony to what the Spirit can do) trusting that he can be led into more and more truth by the Spirit, whose purpose is to glorify Jesus. "When the Spirit of truth comes, he will guide you into all the truth. . . . He will glorify me, because he will take what is mine and declare it to you" (16:13–14). The Prologue is perhaps the most obvious example of the fuller truth John has come into, through and beyond the Synoptics. This is writing in the Spirit, going deeper and deeper into the meaning, the *logos*, that has shaped all reality. This writing, as we mentioned at the end of chapter 1, is a doxological practice, a model for Christian theology, stretching to do justice to "his glory, . . . full of grace and truth" and to "his fullness . . . , grace upon grace" (1:14, 16). Reading it too is a doxological practice, and we will soon attempt to go deeper into the character of this reading.

First, however, the final sentence of John's Gospel needs to be savored. "But there are also many other things that Jesus did; if every one of them were written down, I suppose that the world itself could not contain the books that would be written" (21:25). This is the culminating note of abundance in a Gospel of abundance and fullness. Through the Gospel we find abundant wine, water, bread, life, light, healing, fruitfulness, joy, and love. The Spirit is a wind that blows where it will and is given "without measure" (3:34). And embracing all, framing the whole Gospel, is God and God's glory, seen in Jesus Christ, testified to in John's writing in the Spirit, and read by us who are being given the inexhaustibly abundant gift of this glory. This ending "is the ultimate warning against any definitive, conclusive attempt to sum up, wrap up, comprehend, tie down, or write down what Jesus has done, let alone what he continues to do and, above

6. On authorship, see Ford, *Gospel of John*, 429–31.

all, who he is."[7] It is also an invitation to be guided further, like the author, by the Spirit into more truth, and even to write down what is discovered. Hence this book! But before any such writing comes reading and reread-ing, to which we now turn.

Reading and Rereading, Meeting and Indwelling: All in the Presence of Jesus

The profound simplicity at the heart of reading the Gospel of John is the "I am" of Jesus. Jesus is the one who is as God is, the free and loving self-expression and self-giving of God to us. So Jesus is present to the reader as God is present.

To trust that one is reading in the invisible presence of the person about whom one is reading changes the experience of reading. That trust becomes the experience of meeting through reading (or through being read to, hearing what has been written). John's Gospel is crafted, as are the Synoptic Gospels, around face-to-face meetings with Jesus. Stories of encounters with Jesus are the main way readers (or hearers) are in-troduced to Jesus. To believe that the main character of the stories is present as God is present, open to living interaction, to mutual recep-tivity in love—for the reader, that is to be in a unique, life-changing, all-encompassing relationship. John's insistence throughout the Gospel that this means being in relationship with the glory of God (as the pre-vious section has shown) makes sure that the awesomeness as well as the intimacy of it is realized. One can both be a friend of Jesus and, with Thomas, cry out in worship, "My Lord and my God!" (John 20:28). Trust, love, friendship, and worship can, in this unique relationship, come together.

John has various ways of bringing home to readers the distinctiveness of this relationship. One way is to give a framework of time and eternity, with Jesus being utterly in the world of his time yet also transcending it as God transcends it. He emphasizes this right from the start:

> He was in the beginning with God. . . . John testified to him and cried out, "This was he of whom I said, 'He who comes after me ranks ahead of me

7. Ford, *Gospel of John*, 418.

because he was before me.' . . . After me comes a man who ranks ahead of me because he was before me." (John 1:2, 15, 30)[8]

It recurs through the rest of the Gospel, perhaps most dramatically when Jesus says, "Very truly, I tell you, before Abraham was, I am" (8:58). It is in prayer, above all, that the eternal relationship of Jesus with his Father is clearest: "So now, Father, glorify me in your own presence with the glory that I had in your presence before the world existed" (17:5).

That prayer is also a good example of John's concern to testify both to the pre-resurrection Jesus and to the post-resurrection Jesus in as integrated and simultaneous a way as possible. The prayer's timing is on the night before his death, but Jesus speaks both from there and from a post-resurrection perspective, as when he says, "And now I am no longer in the world" (17:11). The resurrection of Jesus is explicitly anticipated from early in the Gospel (beginning with 2:13–22). John's overwhelming concern with who Jesus is, exemplified in his "I am" sayings but also seen in the way every chapter is concerned with who he is, means that the pre-resurrection Jesus often speaks in ways that assume his resurrection and his eternal relationship with his Father. This can be disconcerting for those who want a historical account that does not make those assumptions. For John, it is about doing justice to the truth of this unique person, whose full identity requires those assumptions. Glory is perhaps the most encompassing concept he uses to integrate the life, death, and resurrection of Jesus with the relationship of Jesus to his Father.

John does not assume that a first reading will result in trusting, let alone indwelling. The text can be read as a pedagogy designed to draw readers into meeting Jesus, and on into trusting him fully. The goal is that of mutual indwelling in love—the overflowing, lasting life whose indescribable depth, intimacy, and intensity are signaled (above all in the prayer of Jesus in John 17) through the mutual glorifying that is prior to creation and is both its deepest secret and its fulfillment in utter joy. But entering into this takes time. The text we read now seems to bear the marks of long, slow meditation, steeped in prayer and the life of discipleship in community. It distills, from the many other texts and testimonies that

---

8. John's repetitions (often they are repetitions with slight variations) are worth noting well, as they tend to be points on which we should spend more time.

are mentioned in John 20:30 and 21:25, what its author and others in his community (among whom is the mother of Jesus) have slowly come to consider the essentials—essential for meeting with Jesus, trusting him, and abiding in him. John is realistic about the range of responses to Jesus that are possible, and part of his pedagogy is to show these and invite the reader to learn from them and decide between them. The drama includes examples of incredulity, bewilderment, misunderstanding, doubt, partial understanding and partial trust, indecision, bitter opposition, denial, betrayal, and wholehearted trust, understanding, and love. The two most vivid instances of step-by-step learning, leading to full trust in Jesus, are perhaps the Samaritan woman at the well in John 4 and the man born blind in John 9.

In John 4 the steps through which the woman and her community recognize who Jesus is and come to believe in him include the following:

- "... you, a Jew" (v. 9);
- "Are you greater than our ancestor Jacob?" (v. 12);
- "Sir, I see that you are a prophet" (v. 19);
- "The woman said to him, 'I know that Messiah is coming' (who is called Christ). 'When he comes, he will proclaim all things to us.' Jesus said to her, 'I am he' [the Greek is simply *egō eimi*, "I am"]" (vv. 25–26);
- "Come and see a man who told me everything I have ever done! He cannot be the Messiah, can he?" (v. 29);
- and the culmination: "We know that this is truly the Savior of the world" (v. 42).

The theme of glory is not explicit in this chapter, but it is implied in the emphasis on worship. "Woman, believe me, the hour is coming when you will worship the Father neither on this mountain nor in Jerusalem. . . . But the hour is coming, and is now here, when the true worshipers will worship the Father in spirit and truth" (4:21, 23). The Jerusalem worship was centered on the glory of God in the temple; here, as in John 2:13–22, Jesus is central.

In John 9 the journey into recognition, trust, and commitment includes a similar series of steps:

- "Rabbi" (v. 2);
- "I am the light of the world" (v. 5);
- "The man called Jesus made mud. . . . Then I went and washed and received my sight" (v. 11);
- "He is a prophet" (v. 17);
- "If this man were not from God, he could do nothing" (v. 33);
- and the culmination: "'Do you believe in the Son of Man?' . . . He said, 'Lord, I believe.' And he worshiped him" (vv. 35, 38).

The theme of glory is explicit in this chapter when the opponents of Jesus challenge the man born blind: "Give glory to God! We know that this man [Jesus] is a sinner" (9:24). But by the end of the story, the way God is being glorified is through "this man" being worshiped.

In each of these chapters, the pedagogy involves far more than the plain sense of the story's progression from a woman or man meeting Jesus to them trusting and believing in him. The way it is written invites re-reading after rereading, enabling continual deepening of understanding. This "deep plain sense" of the text is formed through a convergence of elements.[9] One is the use of capacious symbols and imagery, such as water and food in John 4 or light, sight, and blindness in John 9. Reflection on such imagery is open-ended and inexhaustible and can connect with us in different ways according to what is happening now. The same is true of the repeated use of language whose meaning is enriched as the Gospel unfolds—"glorify" and "glory" are of most interest here, and there are many others, such as *menō* (see above), "life," and "love."

John's characteristic style of writing (it is fascinating to see it reappearing in the Letters of John, especially 1 John) also encourages cross-reference within the Gospel, and there are many examples where we are clearly meant to find more meaning in the light of what comes later, thus requiring rereading. So "we have seen his glory" in John 1:14 is a headline for the rest of the Gospel, and we can return to find further meaning in it (and in the whole Prologue, to which it is central) after each sign, after the Farewell Discourses, and, above all, after the crucifixion and resurrection. Indeed, if we want to read ourselves more and more deeply into

9. On deep plain sense in the Gospel of John and other Scriptures, see Ford, *Gospel of John*, 1, 27, 49, 55, 60, 71, 76–78, 92, 104, 271, 276, 388–91, 434.

this Gospel of glory, we would be wise to develop the habit of rereading (more than once) the whole Gospel in relation to each major reference to glorifying and glory. Those who do this testify to its fruitfulness.

Then there are the resonances of John's text with other texts. The very first words of the Gospel repeat the opening of John's own Bible in its Greek translation, the Septuagint: "In the beginning" (Gen. 1:1; John 1:1). The rest of his text is steeped in the Septuagint. To read that text doxologically is to find the text of John being endlessly enriched, as each rereading generates further light. In this chapter we will concentrate especially on the Psalms,[10] but other books too allow for similar intertextual enrichment. The abundance of meaning in John when read by itself is increased yet further when John is read in conversation with the Septuagint. This of course applies to texts where the theme of glory is explicit. But it goes much further. For example, in 1:14 "we have seen his glory" is given further content by what follows, "the glory as of a father's only son, full of grace and truth," encouraging us to connect with what the Septuagint says about fathers, sons, grace, truth, and fullness. A further example (in which glory is not explicitly mentioned) is in the temple scene in 2:13–22, where Jesus "was speaking of the temple of his body" (v. 21). To read the Old Testament/ Hebrew Scriptures/Septuagint on the temple is to understand how vital it is to the theology of divine glory.[11] There are innumerable other examples. And the conversation goes both ways: John's Gospel and the Septuagint are each illuminated further through this sort of reading and rereading.[12]

What about the rest of the New Testament? Scholars differ about whether the author (or authors) of John's Gospel knew other New Testament writings. We think it likely that John knew all the Synoptic Gospels and also the Pauline tradition (on the latter, see on Ephesians below).[13] But by recognizing the authority of the canon of Scripture,[14] the church has encouraged reading them together, whatever their authors knew of the others. It is generally worthwhile to read any Synoptic passage by asking,

10. Daly-Denton, *David in the Fourth Gospel*.

11. N. T. Wright, *History and Eschatology*.

12. Hays, *Echoes of Scripture in the Gospels*. On Hays, intertextuality in John, and reading John, see Ford, "Reading Backwards."

13. For a detailed argument in favor of this, see the study of the feeding of the five thousand (which occurs in all four Gospels) by Stephen Hunt, *Rewriting the Feeding of the Five Thousand*.

14. There are some differences between Christian traditions on the extent of the canon, but the four Gospels and the letters of Paul are always included.

"How is this illuminated by John?" and to read any passage in John by asking, "How is this illuminated by the Synoptics?" To take just one example that is central to the theology of glory, how do the transfiguration stories relate to John, who does not describe this major Synoptic event? This requires at least a whole book, but we will limit ourselves to taking a little further what we have discussed already about the relation of seeing to reading, and leave it to our readers to go further.[15]

The Synoptic Gospels tell of the disciples Peter, James, and John climbing a high mountain and seeing Jesus "transfigured before them, and his clothes became dazzling white. . . . And there appeared to them Elijah with Moses, who were talking with Jesus" (Mark 9:2–4). Matthew writes that Jesus's "face shone like the sun" (17:2). Luke says that they went up the mountain "to pray" and that while Jesus "was praying, the appearance of his face changed," and that Moses and Elijah "appeared in glory and were speaking of his departure [*exodon*, exodus], which he was about to accomplish [*plēroun*, fill, fulfill] at Jerusalem. . . . They saw his glory and the two men who stood with him" (9:28–32). This is Scripture come alive, intertextuality in person—Elijah, Moses, and Jesus in conversation with each other. Matthew and Luke have added to Mark the emphasis on the transfigured face of Jesus. Luke has added to Mark and Matthew a double emphasis on both prayer and glory and has given figural, scriptural content to the conversation, connecting the exodus with what is about to happen in Jerusalem, the fulfillment of Scripture in the death and resurrection of Jesus. So Luke has drawn out the scriptural meaning more explicitly than Mark or Matthew and has identified this with seeing the glory of Elijah, Moses, and Jesus together. To enter into this meaning is to enter the glory of God.

In all three accounts, Peter suggests ("He did not know what to say, for they were terrified" [Mark 9:6]; "not knowing what he said" [Luke 9:33]) that they make three dwellings, or tents, one each for Jesus, Moses, and Elijah. But, again in all three, this prosaic, inappropriate attempt to prolong the time together is ignored and, instead, the climax comes. Matthew describes it in a way that best captures the resonance with the

---

15. As Michael Ramsey shows, the theme of glory gets laced through the Gospel of John. "The glory which in the Synoptics flashes into the story on the mountain is perceived by Saint John to pervade all the words and works of Jesus" (Ramsey, *The Glory of God and the Transfiguration of Christ*, 123).

cloud-enfolded, glorious presence of God as at Mount Sinai, or as evoked in the Psalms: "While he [Peter] was still speaking, suddenly a bright cloud overshadowed them, and from the cloud a voice said, 'This is my Son, the Beloved; with him I am well pleased; listen to him'" (17:5). This is a transition from seeing to not seeing; it is also a transition from seeing to hearing; and, most important of all, it is entry into the glorious, unseen presence of God, revealed by word. What is revealed is the relationship of love at the heart of all reality, that of the Father and the Son. And this indicative affirmation comes with an imperative invitation centered on the word: "listen to him." Each of the three accounts ends with a striking emphasis on seeing "only Jesus" (Mark 9:8), "no one except Jesus himself alone" (Matt. 17:8), and "Jesus . . . alone" (Luke 9:36). It is clear in whom the revelation of God culminates.

So the Synoptics have already turned into written testimony this story of seeing and not seeing, with its oral conversation and hearing. They invite those who have not seen into what we have been describing as doxological reading. What about John?

Assuming (as we do) that John knew of the transfiguration,[16] he can be read as crafting his Gospel so as to allow readers of the Synoptic accounts to go deeper into its meaning. One key feature after another of this Synoptic story is found to be fundamental in John. The relationship of Jesus, as the beloved Son, to the Father runs all through John, beginning with the Prologue, and is far more richly opened up to readers than in the Synoptics. Its fullest revelation is in John 17. The Word of God is John's opening concept and likewise pervades his text in many ways, above all through its identification with Jesus himself. The scriptural intertextuality between Jesus, Elijah, and Moses that is dramatized in the Synoptic story also runs through John's text—John has fewer direct scriptural quotations than the Synoptics but more pervasive resonances. The voice from the cloud affirms the person of Jesus, who he is—"my Son, the beloved"— and this, together with the final focus on "Jesus himself alone," matches John's concern in every chapter with who Jesus is, above all signaled in his distinctive "I am" sayings. Beyond that, John takes up the theme of love more than the Synoptics, and *beloved* is even applied to the disciple closest

---

16. Yet, as already suggested, even if one does not assume this, a canonical understanding of Scripture allows similar conclusions.

to Jesus, to whom the authorship of the Gospel is also ascribed. Then there is the theme of seeing and not seeing, which, as already explored, goes to the heart of John's intention for readers of his Gospel: that those who have not been eyewitnesses may be blessed by reading his Gospel and come to meet, trust, and abide in Jesus.

Reading John 17, Prayer of Glory and Love

In all these ways, John deepens and extends themes shared by the Synoptic transfiguration accounts. Luke makes explicit three further key elements: prayer, the exodus, and glory. In John this brings us back to the prayer of Jesus in John 17. It is prayed on the eve of Jesus's death in the setting of the Passover, which reenacts the exodus. And it opens up the relationship of Jesus and his Father as one of mutual glorifying, its intensity and centrality brought home through glory words (the verb *doxazein* and the noun *doxa* being used five times in the first five verses). It also takes up other themes from the transfiguration stories: the Father's word ("They have kept your word" [v. 6]), listening to Jesus ("The words that you gave to me I have given to them. . . . I have given them your word" [vv. 8, 14]), and the "not seeing" of those who come later and rely on testimony ("I ask not only on behalf of these, but also on behalf of those who will believe in me through their word" [v. 20]).

The culminating verses after this (vv. 20–26) express the ultimate desire (v. 24) of Jesus. It is rooted in the desire to share with those who trust and love him the very relationship of love and glory that is affirmed by the voice of the Father in the transfiguration.

> As you, Father, are in me and I am in you, may they also be in us, so that the world may believe that you have sent me. The glory that you have given me I have given them, so that they may be one, as we are one, I in them and you in me, that they may become completely one, so that the world may know that you have sent me and have loved them even as you have loved me. (John 17:21–23)

Note there the full sharing of the divine glory, a stupendous thought, and that this glory is inseparable from love. At the transfiguration Peter wanted to prolong the experience by making three dwellings; here is envisaged the fulfillment of that desire in permanent and utterly mutual indwelling in glory and love. It promises all those who trust and love Jesus the ultimate fulfillment of seeing his glory. "Father, I desire that those also, whom you have given me, may be with me where I am, to see my glory, which you have given me because you loved me before the foundation of the world" (v. 24). Those who have been blessed in not seeing, and yet having believed, will find the fulfillment of seeing.

But this is no private, personal, or in-group fulfillment. Its horizon is the whole world that God loves, with no timescale attached. *World* occurs sixteen times in this prayer, and the orientation is toward an ongoing drama of deeper involvement in it, for the sake of God's love and glory. "As you have sent me into the world, so I have sent them into the world" (v. 19). That encourages continual reflection on the story of Jesus in the world while it also, through the open "as . . . so . . . ," inspires continual fresh improvisation on it in prayer, thought, and action in the world.

There is much, much more in this prayer.[17] Readers might want, for example, to explore its deep, multiple resonances with the Lord's Prayer at the center of Matthew's account of the Sermon on the Mount (6:9–15)[18] and, through and beyond that, the mutual illumination of the whole Sermon on the Mount when read in conversation with the Farewell Discourses of John 13–17. Within John's Gospel the Prologue is a specially fruitful intertext. Our focus here has been on the transfiguration, the key story of glory in the Synoptic Gospels, in conversation with the theme of glory in John's Gospel, studied as an encouragement to develop and deepen a doxological reading of the whole Bible. Now, having considered our first interlude text, John 17, we turn to our second.

Praying Ephesians, Epistle of Glory

The Letter to the Ephesians can be read as mature theology in the Pauline tradition,[19] just as the Gospel of John can be read as mature theology in

---

17. See Ford, "Ultimate Desire," and Ford, *Gospel of John*, 328–53.

18. See Ford, *Gospel of John*, 332–33, and Cocksworth, *Prayer*, 125–35. The most obvious evocations of glory are in the leading petition, "Hallowed be your name," and in the will or desire (*thelēma*) of God being "done on earth as in heaven"—those little words *as* and *in* are at the heart of the climax of the prayer of Jesus in John 17:20–26, which can be read as the closest conceivable bringing together of earth and heaven in mutual indwelling: "As you, Father, are in me, and I am in you, may they also be in us, so that the world may believe that you have sent me" (17:21).

19. See n. 1 above on authorship. For convenience we will call the author Paul.

the tradition of Gospel writing. In John 17 we have found the fullest expression of glory and love on the lips of Jesus in prayer. Central to Ephesians is the author's own prayer in 3:14–21, which likewise expresses a superabundance of glory and love together. This invites glory-centered doxological reading that is inseparable from both glory-centered, doxological praying and, as will emerge, glory-centered, doxological singing—all of them inspired by, and inspiring, glory-centered doxological writing.

There will be more on Ephesians in the next chapter, where the main emphasis will be on the church fully alive together, maturing into the fullness of God's glory through new intimacies of togetherness in time and space. For now we concentrate on how reading Ephesians can shape prayer, which is such a crucial part of that maturing. It is an inexhaustible subject, which we will open up first by reading 3:14–21 as a prayer of glory and love, and then by seeing how the rest of the letter illuminates and deepens this prayer and also acts as a springboard to our third interlude text, Psalm 145. This is an exercise in learning to pray by learning to read doxologically.

Praying Ephesians 3:14–21, Prayer of Glory and Love

The prayer in Ephesians 3 is offered "before the Father, from whom every family in heaven and on earth takes its name," and is prayed "according to the riches of his glory" (vv. 14–16). So the glory of God is the framing reality and basic orientation of the prayer. This flows into what follows, the prayer for the readers to be "strengthened in your inner being with power through his Spirit, and that Christ may dwell in your hearts through faith, as you are being rooted and grounded in love" (vv. 16–17). The glory is inseparable from love, just as the Spirit and Jesus Christ are inseparable from the Father, and these lead into the daring desire "that you may be filled with all the fullness of God" (v. 19). But first this fullness is described in terms of the multidimensional "love of Christ," whose "breadth and length and height and depth" stretch the powers of comprehension of the whole community ("all the saints"). This is a love that both is known and "surpasses knowledge" (vv. 18–19).

It might seem that nothing could exceed what has just been prayed for, "all the fullness of God." But this is the fullness of the living, glorious God, infinitely generative and abundant, endlessly rich in wisdom, love, and creativity, whose perfection is dynamic, overflowing, and capaciously hospitable. So there can be a culminating ascription of *glory* to God, "who by the power at work within us is able to accomplish abundantly far more than all we can ask or imagine" (v. 20). The prayer has already affirmed faith and love; this adds an expansive hope beyond anything we might be able to imagine or put into words. The prayer's opening related "every family in heaven and on earth" to God as Father and went on to open up "the riches of his glory"; now, in its climax, the prayer returns "to him . . . to him" (vv. 20–21), and the one word summing up both the reality of God and the fullness God shares with us is *glory*. God's future for us is better than anything we could ever think up for ourselves, and it is a glory that can be the reality of earth and heaven together, in a community of love, in both time and eternity: "To him be glory in the church and in Christ Jesus to all generations, forever and ever. Amen" (v. 21).

It is a prayer that has been read and prayed repeatedly for nearly two thousand years, and this continues around the world today. It is sometimes prayed as a whole, often in excerpts, and it is frequently improvised on, extempore or in liturgies, collects, and other prayers. It invites into

- physical involvement ("I bow my knees");
- global and transgenerational solidarity ("every family in heaven and on earth," "all generations");
- rich interiority ("in your inner being," "power at work within us");
- the opening of hearts in trust to Jesus Christ ("that Christ may dwell in your hearts through faith");
- being loved and loving as utterly fundamental ("being rooted and grounded in love");[20]
- the stretching of minds in a community of learners ("the power to comprehend, with all the saints, . . . the breadth and length and height and depth");
- recognition of a reality that exceeds all our mind's cognitive capacities but can actually be received by us ("the love of Christ that surpasses knowledge," "all the fullness of God");

20. Note the combination of the living, dynamic imagery of being "rooted" and the solid, stable imagery of being "grounded" (*tethemeliōmenoi*, from *themelios*, a building's foundation or foundation stone).

- confidence in the unlimited generosity and future blessings of God, far exceeding our most daring hopes and prayers ("abundantly far more than all we can ask or imagine");
- and taking all of this up into worshiping and glorifying God ("To him be glory").

Together, that all amounts to an invitation into full Christian maturity as something that is never complete, because it is a life of more and more glorifying, learning, and loving, always open to the unimaginable surprises of God.

The Prayer and the Rest of the Letter

By the time readers of Ephesians arrive at the prayer in chapter 3, they have been offered a whole God-centered ecology within which to understand God, themselves, their life in community, and creation. It is an ecology of blessing. "Blessed be the God and Father of our Lord Jesus Christ, who has blessed us in Christ with every spiritual blessing in the heavenly places" (1:3). Blessing, in the context of the rest of Scripture, and especially the Psalms, is closely associated with glorifying, praising, thanking, rejoicing, adoring, magnifying, sanctifying. Blessing circulates through the dynamic interrelationships of this ecology, as God blesses human beings and creation, creatures bless God, and human beings can bless God, creation, and each other. In Ephesians 1 the blessing is centered inseparably on God the Father and Jesus Christ, and on "us," a community whose character will be explored in our next chapter. For now, the vital element is the repeated overflow into doxology: "to the praise of his glorious grace that he freely bestowed on us in the Beloved . . . according to the riches of his grace that he lavished on us . . . so that we . . . might live for the praise of his glory . . . marked with the seal of the promised Holy Spirit; this is the pledge of our inheritance toward redemption as God's own people, to the praise of his glory" (1:6–14).

Those "riches of his grace" correlate with the "riches of his glorious inheritance among the saints" (Eph. 1:18), the "immeasurable riches of his grace in kindness toward us in Christ Jesus" (2:7), and "the news of the boundless riches of Christ" (3:8), and all flow into the "riches of his glory" in the central prayer (3:16). Receiving and acknowledging these riches inspires ceaseless thanks in the author (1:16) and should do so in the community (5:20). This prayer and praise stretches the mind ("all wisdom and insight" [1:8]) as well as the heart and imagination. Above all, it is our desire that is being inspired, energized, reoriented.

The very first sentence of the letter is "Paul, an apostle of Christ Jesus by the will of God" (Eph. 1:1). The Greek word for "will" is *thelēma*, which means "desire" as much as "will." This is important to remember, partly because through Christian history there have often been meanings attached to "the will of God" which imply that it is coercive, eliminating any freedom of human response. "Desire" allows for the importance of the letter's urgent appeals ("I . . . beg you" [4:1]; "Let all of us . . ." [4:25]; "Do not grieve the Holy Spirit" [4:30]; "Live in love, as Christ loved us and gave himself up for us" [5:2]; and many more) and its core concern that our desires harmonize with God's ("Try to find out what is pleasing to the Lord" [5:10]).

The deepest, most comprehensive shaping and expression of our desire is through prayer, as the culminating appeal makes clear.

> Pray in the Spirit at all times in every prayer and supplication. To that end keep alert and always persevere in supplication for all the saints. Pray also for me, so that when I speak, a message may be given to me to make known with boldness [*en parrhēsia*] the mystery of the gospel, for which I am an ambassador in chains. Pray that I may declare it boldly [*parrhēsiasōmai*], as I must speak. (Eph. 6:18–20)

Parrhēsia is confident and free communication, overflowing and public (what Jesus in the Gospel of John says he has been doing [18:20]), inviting free response. It is the sort of communication that is most in tune with the ecology of blessing, praise, and thanks; with "the mystery of the gospel" (Eph. 6:19); and with "the mystery of his [God's] will [or desire]" (1:9).

In the rich lead-up to the prayer in Ephesians 3, there is repeated emphasis (3:3, 4, 9) on this mystery of superabundant grace, wisdom ("the wisdom of God in its rich variety" [3:10]), and love, summed up as "the mystery of Christ" (3:4). Moreover, this is connected with writing and reading: "how the mystery was made known to me by revelation, as I wrote above in a few words, a reading of which will enable you to perceive my understanding of the mystery of Christ" (3:3–4). In our terms, this is doxological writing and reading. Like the writing of the Gospel of John so that those who have not been eyewitnesses can respond to Jesus through reading (as discussed above), so here the written testimony to Paul's revelation attracts readers into the mystery of Christ. In him "we have access to God in boldness [*parrhēsia*] and confidence through faith in him" (3:12). The stage is set for the written performance of *parrhēsia* according to the riches of God's glory in 3:14–21, enabling generations of readers to participate and improvise further.

Yet there is one more crucial thing. The final statement of the actual written lead-in to praying Ephesians 3:14–21 is a prayer before that prayer. "I pray therefore that you may not lose heart over my sufferings for you; they are your glory [*doxa*]" (3:13). At the heart of the letter's headline opening doxology was the death of Jesus. "In him we have redemption through his blood, the forgiveness of our trespasses, according to the riches of his grace that he lavished on us" (1:7–8). In Ephesians 2 the death of Jesus is the event through which Jews and gentiles (who together make up all humanity) are brought together, their alienation and hostility overcome. They have been "brought near by the blood of Christ. For he is our peace; in his flesh he has made both groups into one and has broken down the dividing wall, that is, the hostility between us . . . that he might create in himself one new humanity in place of the two, thus making peace, and might reconcile both groups to God in one body through the cross, thus putting to death that hostility through it" (2:13–16). Now, as he prepares to pray for his readers, the sufferings of the writer for the readers are identified with glory. Desire for God and for God's glory is inseparable from realism about the cost of identifying with the glory of God as embodied in Jesus Christ: this is a way that cannot avoid suffering.

So, just as the last mention of glory in the Gospel of John is about Peter glorifying God by suffering and dying (21:18–19), here the naming of the writer's suffering for others as "glory" is the last mention of glory before the glory-suffused prayer that follows (and after that there is no further explicit reference to glory in Ephesians). The realism about sin, suffering, and evil continues through the second half of the letter. There are warnings and exhortations to the fallible Christian community, which is clearly vulnerable to sins and distractions of many sorts, and there is a call to spiritual warfare, followed by that urgent encouragement, already discussed, to "pray in the Spirit at all times" (Eph. 6:18).

The most vivid exhortation opens with a call to be wise and realize what God's desire is: "So do not be foolish, but understand what the will [desire, *thelēma*] of the Lord is" (Eph. 5:17). This desire is for doxology: "Do not get drunk with wine, for that is debauchery; but be filled with the Spirit, as you sing psalms and hymns and spiritual songs among yourselves, singing and making melody to the Lord in your hearts, giving thanks to God the Father at all times and for everything in the name of our Lord Jesus Christ" (5:18–20).[21] That is a good springboard into the Psalms themselves.

Singing Psalm 145, Poetry of Glory

The deepest root of the language of glory in the Gospel of John and in the Letter to the Ephesians is in the book of Psalms. Their authors, like Jesus, were immersed in the Psalms, and the way of life into which they invite readers is one in which praying and singing the Psalms is habitual. Doxological reading and doxological praying inspire and are inspired by doxological praising and singing. To become fluent in glorifying God is to speak the language of the Psalms. Century after century, and around the world today, both Jews and Christians have learned this wisdom.

Psalm 145 is the psalm of psalms, an incomparable expression of pure praise, pure doxology. Ellen F. Davis, a profound contemporary interpreter and translator of the Psalms, writes, "Psalm 145 is the climactic point in the Psalter, and the heading marks its singular status. Although the Hebrew title for the Psalter as a whole is *Tehillim*, 'Praisings,' this is the only individual psalm that is designated *tehillah*, 'a praising.'"[22] Her new translation of it is the doxological interlude following chapter 3.

It is an ecology of blessing and glory that has a supreme concentration on praising God for who God is. It opens with the individual "I" of the psalmist repeatedly lifting up "Your name forever and ever"; it closes with "all flesh" blessing "His holy Name forevermore." So, who God is fills all time,[23] a message intensified by "every day I bless You," "generation to generation," "Your governance in every single generation," "long in patience," and "sovereignty through all ages."

21. See Ford, *Self and Salvation*, 107–36.
22. Davis, Fujimura, and Held, *Light within Light* (forthcoming).
23. See below, chap. 3.

Yet it is not only all time: "all" is in the Hebrew no less than eighteen times. All people, all life, and all that God has created also play their part in this praise: "All Your works acclaim You, O ADONAI, and those true to You bless You!" The glory of God as God and king—"the glorious splendor of Your majesty . . . the glory of Your sovereignty . . . the glorious splendor of Your sovereignty"—is exemplified in all God's words and works, and all together show who God is, God's intrinsic character and perfection. God is a God of "lavish goodness [and] righteousness. . . . Faithful is ADONAI in all His words and covenant-committed in all His works. . . . Righteous is ADONAI in all His ways and covenant-true in all His doings."

In terms of the language of Ephesians, this is the poetry of *parrhēsia*— abundant, overflowing exultation, and celebration of the glory of God. Poetry, as Davis writes, "is 'maximal speech'—condensed, intentional, rhythmic language, meant to get into the body and deep memory. The combination of words and rhythm, especially when accompanied by music and physical movements, gives poetry the potential for unlocking emotions that discursive or imaginative language cannot touch."[24] The rest of the Psalms exemplify this in many ways, across a full spectrum of human experience, good and bad.[25] In Psalm 145, "absent are the cries of lament, prayers of petition and even thanksgiving that occupy so many psalmists; now all that is left is pure, self-forgetful praise. This is the mode of prayer traditionally known as adoration, whose sole purpose is to render to God what is God's alone: the acknowledgment of incomparability, 'the glorious splendor of [divine] majesty' (v. 5)."[26]

24. Davis, *Opening Israel's Scriptures*, 313, citing Steiner, *After Babel*, 233.

25. For a recent example of such poetry, see O'Siadhail, *Testament*, which has 150 new psalms and fifty retellings of New Testament stories in poetry in a variety of forms. In her endorsement of the book, Ellen Davis says this:

> Love and prayer are the intertwined themes of every poem in this book, which demonstrates that praising God well is less a spontaneous act than the work of a lifetime spent in faith. O'Siadhail shares the Psalmists' unapologetic subjectivity, the immediacy of their prayer, their insistence on the actuality of a loving relationship with God, perceived in part through suffering. Here the mature poet prays for "years to leave love's legacy behind," and this book is part of the fulfilment of his wise desire.

Abundant glory is a key theme in O'Siadhail's Psalter (146):

Your glory overflows its brim.

All that is calls us to you. (*Testament*, 153)

As they were being written, these new psalms were shared by Micheal O'Siadhail as we were writing this book, as were our draft chapters with him.

26. Davis, Fujimura, and Held, *Light within Light* (forthcoming).

This adoration points to a deep truth of our relationship with God. God is to be adored for God's sake, because of who God is, simply because "great is Adonai and highly praiseworthy." Of course, the character of God means that blessings pour out on all creatures. But these blessings are not the root reason for blessing and praising God. This is not a quid pro quo relationship, and there are pivotal, challenging moments in the Bible when this is devastatingly clear.

At the start of Israel's covenantal history with God, "God tested Abraham" (Gen. 22:1) by telling him to sacrifice his only son, Isaac. Would Abraham trust, honor, and obey God even when it meant losing "your only son Isaac, whom you love," the sign of God's blessing (22:2)? Would he do this for God's sake? Abraham's utter trust in God is at the root of Israel's covenantal relationship. "By myself I have sworn, says the Lord: Because you have done this, and have not withheld your son, your only son, I will indeed bless you, and I will make your offspring as numerous as the stars of heaven and as the sand that is on the seashore" (22:16–17).

At the opening of the book of Job, another test situation is set up in an exchange between God and Satan. The key question, to which all the rest of the book can be read as a response,[27] is asked by Satan: "Does Job fear God for nothing?" (Job 1:9).[28] The Septuagint translation of "for nothing" is *dōrean*, "as a gift, freely," implying: Does Job relate to God for God's sake, because of who God is? In terms of Psalm 145, will Job continue to "bless Your name forever and ever" even when he is not experiencing God's "lavish goodness . . . covenant-love . . . compassion . . . love"? Job has many blessings: children, wealth, health, social standing and respect, friends, religious comfort, and more. Satan asks whether his relationship with God will survive the loss of such blessings: "Have you not put a fence around him and his house and all that he has, on every side? You have blessed the work of his hands, and his possessions have increased in the land. But stretch out your hand now, and touch all that he has, and he will curse you to your face" (Job 1:10–11). In what follows, Job, like Abraham, stays faithful: "Though he slay me, yet will I trust in him" (13:15 KJV).

---

27. On this, see Ticciati, *Job and the Disruption of Identity*. See also Ford, *Christian Wisdom*, 90–120 (for discussion of Job) and 121–52 (for "Job and Post-Holocaust Wisdom").

28. "Fearing God" is a phrase that embraces the whole relationship of trusting, knowing, honoring, worshiping, obeying, loving, and fearing God.

Davis follows Psalm 145 through Jewish history and its many Job-like experiences:

> Coming at the end of the Psalter, the overflowing praise of this poem appears as an act of resilience and resistance, pitting the glory of God's sovereignty as a force more than equal to all the evil and injustice and grief of the world. Through a lifetime and "generation to generation" (Ps. 145:4), the tough practice of self-forgetful praise enables love and faith to endure—and as rabbinic tradition understands it, even beyond this lifetime. The Talmud affirms that anyone who recites this "praising" of David three times each day will have a place in the world-to-come (BT Berakhot 4b), and that dictum remains formative for Jewish liturgy and prayer.[29] From the Crusades to the pogroms to the Nazi ghettos and death camps, Psalm 145 has been repeated daily by millions subjected to the cruelest forms of hegemony, countering with the bold assertion that the Eternal will ultimately defeat every vicious assertion of power: ". . . all the wicked He annihilates" (Ps. 145:20).[30]

In the Gospel of John there are headline statements in the Prologue: "The light shines in the darkness, and the darkness did not overcome it. . . . And the Word became flesh and lived among us, and we have seen his glory, the glory as of a father's only son, full of grace and truth" (1:5, 14). It is in "the hour," on the verge of the crucifixion, the darkest moment in the story, that Jesus prays John 17, which opens up the depths of the glory of God (see above). The preparation for understanding the character of this glory has been given all through the Gospel and has intensified in John 12, followed by the Farewell Discourses.

Jesus announces, "The hour has come for the Son of Man to be glorified" (John 12:23), and that glorifying is centered on the crucifixion of Jesus. It is a strange truth: "Very truly, I tell you, unless a grain of wheat falls into the earth and dies, it remains just a single grain; but if it dies, it bears much fruit" (12:24). It is a truth that calls for utter, Abrahamic or Job-like trust in God. Jesus himself is agonized by the prospect—-"Now my soul is troubled"—but his response resonates with the opening and closing verses of Psalm 145: "Father, glorify your name" (12:27–28). The

---

29. Psalm 145 forms the core of the Ashrei prayer, which in traditional congregations is recited twice in the morning service and once in the afternoon service.

30. Davis, Fujimura, and Held, *Light within Light* (forthcoming).

glorifying of God's name is the deepest meaning of the whole Gospel, and this is immediately confirmed by the only voice from heaven in the Gospel of John: "I have glorified it, and I will glorify it again" (12:28). The resonances with Psalm 145 continue with the confident assertion of the overcoming of evil and, above all, the climactic prediction by Jesus: "And I, when I am lifted up from the earth, will draw all people ["all things" in some good manuscripts] to myself" (12:32). That resonates not only with the multiple uses of "all" in Psalm 145; in addition, the Greek verb for "lifted up" is the same as the Septuagint uses in the first verse of Psalm 145, "I will exalt You, my God." The lifting up on the cross and the glorifying of God's name are inseparable, and the prayer of Jesus in John 17 takes readers deeper into this.

But first come the Farewell Discourses, alongside which Psalm 145 can also be read fruitfully. Of the many possible points of mutual illumination—such as on prayer, joy, the name, righteousness, truth, desire, protection[31]—we will focus on just one: the relationship between greatness and love.

Psalm 145 has overwhelming affirmations of God's greatness and affirms God as loving and also compassionate, good, gracious, long-suffering, faithful, generous, and having other love-related qualities. It is clear that God's kingship, greatness, and power are not coercive or tyrannical but in line with justice and love. In particular, "ADONAI is supporting all who are fallen and raising up all who have collapsed" (Ps. 145:14).[32] The Farewell Discourses reconceive not only glory but also, inseparably, greatness and love. "So if I, your Lord and Teacher, have washed your feet, you also ought to wash one another's feet. . . . Very truly, I tell you, servants are not greater than their master, nor are messengers greater than the one who sent them" (John 13:14, 16). This leads

---

31. On each of these in the Farewell Discourses, see Ford, *Gospel of John*: on prayer, 269–70, 280–83, 294, 297, 301–13, 328–34, 338–47, 349, 350, 352, 380; on joy, 253, 290, 296–97, 309, 311, 318–21, 343, 352; on the name, 252, 269–70, 275–76, 280–81, 284, 288, 300–304, 308–9, 315, 318–21, 328–38, 341–47, 353; on righteousness, 303, 311, 313, 353; on truth, 275–77, 285, 312–18, 343–45; on desire, 294, 297, 313, 328–29, 346–48, 352; on protection, 329, 338, 341–42.

32. Cf. the final lines of the final psalm in O'Siadhail's Psalter (150):
Grant us now grace to dare
Your evolution's fresh demand:
To love the weak your love's finesse. (*Testament*, 158)

on into Jesus giving "a new commandment, that you love one another. Just as I have loved you, you also should love one another" (13:34). It is greatness centered on humble service, and love modeled on Jesus, with God-centered glorifying as its context: "Jesus said, 'Now the Son of Man has been glorified, and God has been glorified in him. If God has been glorified in him, God will also glorify him in himself and will glorify him at once'" (13:31–32). And later, unsurpassable greatness in love is seen in the crucifixion of Jesus: "No one has greater love than this, to lay down one's life for one's friends" (15:13). That is where the glory and greatness of God are enacted in incomparable love.

The heart of this love is then revealed in the prayer of Jesus in John 17, as explored above. There remains one final insight, perhaps the most important of all. The desire of Jesus in that prayer is for utter mutuality in glorifying and loving, for which the condition is utter, freely given trust. This is the truth of love: it cannot be coerced, and even the greatness and power of God cannot force a response in trust and love. If it were forced, it would not be love, just as praise that is forced does not ring true. Jesus, God in vulnerable flesh, is vulnerable to misunderstanding, rejection, denial, betrayal, torture, and execution. His desire is for full, trusting, joyful, glorious mutuality, but the only way this can happen is if he is received in trust and love.

We conclude this chapter with Micheal O'Siadhail's retelling in poetry of the climactic overcoming of distrust in the Gospel of John, together with its surprise conclusion, the blessing of us readers:

> Thomas, who's called the twin, was absent when
> Jesus had come and shown his hands and side.
>
> There in a locked room he'd said to them again,
> "Peace to you all." But Thomas told replied:
>
> "If I don't finger myself the nail-pierced hands,
> Till I can poke inside his wound, I cannot trust."
>
> After eight weeks among them Jesus stands
> Saying to Thomas "finger my palms and thrust
>
> Deeply your hand into my wound. Don't doubt!"
> Now what's the need to touch or feel or prod,

Insert a hand? All faithlessness crossed out,
Thomas declares at once: "My Lord and my God."

Sceptical twin that all of us have been,
Nail marks and side-wound unseen, are we deceived?

"Thomas, you have believed because you've seen;
Blessed who have not seen and have believed."[33]

33. O'Siadhail, "Thomas," in *Testament*, 218.

DOXOLOGICAL INTERLUDE

Ephesians 3:14–21

For this reason I bow my knees before the Father, from whom every family in heaven and on earth takes its name. I pray that, according to the riches of his **glory** [*doxēs*], he may grant that you may be strengthened in your inner being with power through his Spirit, and that Christ may dwell in your hearts through **faith** [*pisteōs*, trust and belief], as you are being rooted and grounded in love [*en agapē*]. I pray that you may have the power [*exischysēte*, or "you may be **fully** able"] to comprehend, **with** [*syn*] all the saints, what is the breadth and length and height and depth, and to know the love [*agapēn*] of Christ that surpasses [*hyperballousan*] knowledge, so that you may be **filled** [*plērōthēte*] with all the **fullness** [*plērōma*] of God.

Now to him who by the power at work within us is able to accomplish abundantly far more [*hyperekperissou*] than all we can ask or imagine, to him be **glory** [*doxa*] in the church and in Christ Jesus to all generations, forever and ever. Amen.

CHAPTER THREE

The Church Fully Alive

THE DOCTRINE OF GLORIFICATION, as the most ecumenical of doctrines, needs to be approached ecumenically and invites ecumenical engagement around what really matters. Indeed, a theological theme so weighty as glory can be approached *only* ecumenically—in the broadest terms possible, with multidirectional openness to receive from others, especially from those who have come to experience glory differently, something of what it means to glorify God. As Mayra Rivera puts it, we are called to seek glory "with feeble words and images to express the inexpressible, in a multiplicity of voices, languages, and genres."[1] Everyone catches sight of glory partially, through differently angled clefts in differently positioned rocks. And the glory of God stirs you to move beyond the edges of your own ecclesial perspectives to seek what others have said about glory; and the more you look, the more there is to be found. It would not be too much of an exaggeration to say that every major tradition in every period of the church's history has been committed to the serious study of glory, each resonating with glory in different ways, each finding new dimensions to glory, each with gifts to share. Only together do we gain a fuller sense of what glory entails. Even then, glory exceeds the combined efforts of different theologies, and extends beyond them too, inspiring ongoing, never-finished, and always-seeking doxological

---

1. Rivera, "Glory," 167.

discoveries. New depths to glory are still being found around the world, as they have been century after century, and will continue to be multiplied further as the glory of God is experienced in fresh ways and in new places.

In chapter 1 we said that glory brings the Nicene Creed fully to life by making a doxology of the creed. In chapter 2 we said that glory brings the practice of reading the Bible, especially reading the Bible doxologically and therefore intertextually, fully to life. Now, in this chapter, and in another play on the Irenaean dictum, we are suggesting that the glory of God makes the church fully alive. *Vivens ecclesia!* We start with a discussion of the creedal mark of unity, showing that the glory of God makes the church not only alive but alive *together*. Then we turn to the Ephesian idea of "fullness" to show that the glory of God makes the church not only alive together but *fully* alive together in time and space. We call this sense of togetherness the "*syn* factor," following the gloriously energetic *syn* prefix first encountered in chapter 1. From there, we explore one practical attempt to bring the church fully alive together, Receptive Ecumenism, and then turn to the doxological life of Pentecostalism, finding especially in the doxology of tarrying a particularly vivacious expression of the church fully alive with the glory of God.

The Church Fully Alive, Fully Together

In many church traditions, at some point during a service of Christian worship, there likely comes a moment when those gathered will pause to say the creed together. After belief in the Father, Son, and Spirit has been affirmed, the congregation turns to confess belief in the "one, holy, catholic, and apostolic Church." These are the marks of the church. Anyone who has spent time in actual churches knows how far the church falls from these things. When we look at the fragmentations, divisions, and wounds of the church, the prospect of the first mark (unity) seems especially inconceivable. However, if glory makes a doxology of the creed, and a richer doxological translation of *pisteuomen* is "we trust," saying the creed as a doxology of trust is more than about believing in the church as it currently is. It is about trusting in God to gather together the church into what it is called to be: the glorified body of Christ, united in holiness, catholicity, and apostolicity. The future orientation of the doctrine of glorification reminds Christians that life as it is, is not life as it could be. Alongside "trust," then, another alternative to "belief" drawn from the repertoire of glory is "desire." Shifting the mood from the imperative to the optative reveals a different tonality to these creedal marks. These marks of the church become cries of desire, the yearning and longing for what we do not yet see, seeing beyond the multiple divisions of the church to desire the holy unity that awaits all things.

It could be tempting to make glory the fifth mark of the church. Just as the order of salvation culminates in glory, so too the marks of the church. However, rather than adding to them, the four marks of the church— individually and together—are intensified by glory, just as the individual stages of the *ordo salutis* are integrated and intensified by glory. If you want to know the signs of the church made fully alive by the glory of God, these are the things you should look for. Where there is unity, there is glory. Where there is holiness, catholicity, and apostolicity, there is more glory. Moreover, glory inspires the church to work toward deeper sorts of unity, holiness, catholicity, and apostolicity. Glory encourages the church to enjoy that work. And glory intensifies each of the marks of the church by making them fully alive in relation to each other. The more the church is united, the holier it is. Once the church is fully these things, and loves to enjoy these things, the more the church is, in a word, glorified—*vivens ecclesia*.

Each of the marks of the church is inseparably important. Holiness is especially important in that it shares with glory a deep concern for the Godness of God. If this were a full-scale ecclesiology, each of the marks would need to be worked through in relation to glory. What the present discussion requires is something more modest, and it follows others by focusing—in dialogue with the Letter to the Ephesians—on the unity of the church as the ultimate mark of the church fully alive.[2] We have taken Ephesians to be the culmination of the Pauline tradition and the most glorious of epistles. Now, in this chapter, we take Ephesians to present the most vibrant ecclesiology of glory with a fundamental concern with what is ultimate for the church.

Ephesians takes epistolary form, but it begins in doxology and the overall dynamic is formational. The desire is for the building up of a mature

---

2. In *Dogmatic Ecclesiology*, 1:451–52, Tom Greggs shows that unity is the most comprehensive mark of the church and qualifies the call for holiness, catholicity, and apostolicity.

church together, over the long haul, into fuller participation in the glory of God. The probable origins of the letter lie in doxological performance—in eucharistic or baptismal setting—and this, as we shall see, is important. Doxology sets the overall tone of the letter ("Blessed be the God and Father of our Lord Jesus Christ" [1:3]; "I do not cease to give thanks for you" [1:16]) and emerges as the overriding practical wisdom for what makes a church fully alive in Christ, ending with the great imperative to "pray in the Spirit at all times in every prayer and supplication" (6:18). What is being asked of Christians is that they gather together, and when together they pray together.

Throughout, Paul encourages doxology as the most important thing a community can do by exemplifying it. In the opening doxology he prays,

> With all wisdom and insight he has made known to us the mystery of his will [*thelēmatos*], according to his good pleasure that he set forth in Christ, as a plan for the fullness [*plērōmatos*] of time, to gather up all things in him, things in heaven and things on earth. (Eph. 1:8–10)

This is a vast vision with inexhaustible dimensions that brings everything—including, but cosmically more than, the church—together. It suggests that the unity of the church as the body of Christ is not confined to the global; it is a catholicity that extends to everything. The most embracing idea in Ephesians, then, is the gathering up of everything in Christ to the "glorification of God's glory," to use Hans Urs von Balthasar's translation of 1:6.[3] This is God's ultimate desire. The ultimate calling of the church is to be attracted into the desire of God, to let desires be shaped in line with it, and to desire what God desires. The ultimate desire of the church is unity, for this is the ultimate mystery of God's desire revealed in Jesus Christ.

The Syn Factor

The fundamental call to ecclesial "togetherness" is intensified in Ephesians 2:4–6 through the lavish piling up of the most energizing Greek verbs, each led by the dazzlingly glorious *syn* prefix.

---

3. Balthasar, *The Glory of the Lord*, 6:41.

> God, who is rich in mercy, out of the great love with which he loved us
> even when we were dead through our trespasses, made us alive together
> [*synezōopoiēsen*] with Christ . . . and raised us up [*synēgeiren*] with him and
> seated us [*synekathisen*] with him in the heavenly places in Christ Jesus.

Syn upon *syn* upon *syn*. The *syn* prefix features throughout Ephesians and
is there too in the Nicene Creed. In the pneumatology article, we recall
from chapter 1, the Nicene Creed affirms the divinity of the Spirit because
the Spirit is glorified "with" (*syndoxazomenon*) the Father and the Son.[4]
As in the Nicene Creed, so too in Ephesians, the prefix suggests total
togetherness. Something of the significance of the Greek can be felt in
the English word *synergy*: the interaction that comes from when two or
more are gathered produces a combined energy greater than the sum of
their separate effects. The prefix brings verbs already full of life *more* fully
to life. The desire of God is for us to be, not only made alive, but made
alive together; not only raised up, but raised up together; not only seated
with Christ in heavenly places, but seated together. Could anything be
more compelling, challenging, and imperative than the divine desire for
the church to be made fully alive by being gathered *together* all in all, as
a whole, in Christ?

The maturing into the fullness of God's glory is a deepening into ever
more intensified relations of "togetherness" in ways that surpass knowledge and understanding. Indeed, the utterly joint character of glorification means that divisions within the lives of individual churches cannot
be healed until the separations between churches are overcome, and the
dismantling of these might not be possible until the dividing walls between
the church and other religions are brought down. The more we join in
the flow of glory that moves within the divine life, the more our lives
come to be shaped by the same sort of relationality. It rubs off on us. We
are moved beyond relations of scarcity and competition generated by the
conditions of sin, and we are drawn into the sorts of relations of equality
and mutual intensification as summarized by the doxological "with" of
the Nicene Creed.

---

4. Verbs with the prefix *syn* feature prominently and regularly throughout Ephesians—for
example, in 4:3, where Paul speaks of the bond of peace, and then again in 4:16's discussion
of the body being joined and knit together. Even when *syn-* words are not directly invoked,
such as 1:8–10, the "*syn* factor" should be applied and its logic of togetherness implied.

One God, One Church

Ephesians contains the most comprehensive New Testament statement about the unity of togetherness, given with a *syn-* word thrown in.

> I therefore, the prisoner in the Lord, beg you to lead a life worthy of the calling to which you have been called, with all humility and gentleness, with patience, bearing with one another in love, making every effort to maintain the unity of the Spirit in the bond [*syndesmō*] of peace. There is one body and one Spirit, just as you were called to the one hope of your calling, one Lord, one faith, one baptism, one God and Father of all, who is above all and through all and in all. (Eph. 4:1–6)

The unity of the church does not subsist in some corporate institution, shared declaration showing doctrinal coherence, shared program of practical commitments, or shared patterns of worship. While these practical expressions of unity are vitally important, Ephesians locates the unity of the church in something more fundamental: in the deepest desire of God.

The theme of unity in Ephesians is so utterly centered on God that theology and ecclesiology can be understood only together. The church's journeying deeper into unity is a deepening into ever-deeper experiences of the unity of God. While a good deal of contemporary trinitarian theology is resolute in its emphasis on the threeness of God, in what is probably the most profound return to the divine oneness in recent times, Katherine Sonderegger warns that the doctrine of the Trinity, "however central to the Christian mystery, must not be allowed to replace or silence the Oneness of God. God is supremely, gloriously One; surpassingly, uniquely One."[5] From the first commandment, that besides God there is no other (Deut. 5:6–7), to the Shema and its call to "Hear, O Israel" that "the LORD is our God, the LORD alone" (Deut. 6:4), to Jesus's prayer in John 17:22 to "be one, as we are one," to the Nicene Creed and its intensification of divine monotheism as Holy Trinity, there is nothing more theological than God's holy, glorious unity. The significance of divine unity in the context of the church's desiring of unity is, quite simply, immense: the unity of the church correlates theologically in closest possible terms to the God who is gloriously one and continually at work through the one

---

5. Sonderegger, *Systematic Theology*, 1:xiv.

Spirit, gathering all things into the dynamic of one body, through one calling, in one baptism and one faith. The ultimate desire of God is the "oneing," to use Julian's glorious term, of all things, especially the church.[6]

The prayer of Jesus in John 17, which we have taken to be the ultimate glory text in the Bible, reveals the ultimate desire of Jesus for "oneing." Unusually, in John 17 Jesus discloses to others the content of his prayer: "The glory that you have given me I have given them, so that they may be one as we are one, I in them and you in me, that they may become completely one" (vv. 22–23). Here, the glory of God that flows abundantly in the life of God is shared with the community gathered in the name of Jesus. In chapter 1 we said that "glory" language speaks of the closest possible unity and deepest differentiation within the life of God. Although the Son's glorification of the Father cannot be thought apart from the Father's glorification of the Son, the Son's giving of glory is particular to the Son, as is the Father's to the Father—it is particular and therefore different. The unity of the church rooted in the embracing reality of mutual glorification in the life of God is not, therefore, the sort of unity that flattens difference into a homogeneity where everyone thinks and glorifies God the same way, but one that brings about the closest possible togetherness in the context of an abundance of difference.

Bound up with the theocentric impulses of Ephesians, and its indexing of the unity of the church to the unity of God, is a bias toward divine agency. Paul speaks of "the immeasurable greatness of [God's] power" and "the strength of his power" (Eph. 1:19; 6:10). It takes the power and strength of God, and only this power and strength, to move the church beyond its divisions into the sort of unity that is its chief end. Unity is not, strictly speaking, something the church can predict or control or achieve on its own. It is fully reliant on God's initiative worked out "before the foundation of the world" (1:4). As Tom Greggs says, it is something that "lies ahead of us as we continue to experience the gracious work of God in the realities of space-time: it is something from which and towards which we journey *as the Holy Spirit actualizes the unity of the church as an event.*"[7] If glory relativizes even death, it certainly relativizes the work toward Christian unity. The unity of the church is infinitely more fundamental

---

6. See Julian of Norwich, *Showings.*
7. Greggs, *Dogmatic Ecclesiology,* 1:453.

than the overcoming of the divisions that separate churches from each other and from the world: it is a recognition that the most glorious unity already exists in the abundant simplicity of God. This makes unity a gift before it is a task. It is a stretching into and joining in something that is already in heaven if not yet on earth.

The unity of the church is the ultimate desire of God, of Jesus, and of those who meet in his name. It is ultimate for the church too in the sense of describing a future orientation. Regardless of the particular ordering of what comes before, it is right and proper for there to be glorification at the summit of the various accounts of the *ordo salutis*. Eternal life is being/oneing with the glory of the Father, and the Son, and the Spirit—and this is what the church should be forming people to desire. It is right for conceptions of the Christian life to culminate in the ultimate of glorification because *glory* is a synonym of *unity*: where there is glory, there is unity. However, while there is always an "eschatological note to be sounded," and while glory relativizes the work toward unity, it does not make that work any less imperative for the life of the church today. The dynamics of glory make unity not only teleologically ultimate but also ultimate for the present desire of the church.[8] Working toward the unity of the church is an imperative for the present—the church needs glory hunters, as it were, those actively working toward unity against the odds of the present. Our actions should be determined by this desire and energized by the Spirit, the bond of peace, the ultimate synergizer. The ultimate calling of the church is to image in the world today, however fragmentary and proleptically, the togetherness that awaits all things.

In searching for new ways of conceptualizing the *imago Dei*, there has been a move in theological anthropology away from speaking of the image of God as a noun (something we are or become) to speaking of it as a verb (something we *do*).[9] As a noun, conceptions of the image of God can become excessively static and overly definitional. As a verb, the *imago Dei* is something much more dynamic and relational. The ultimate calling of Christians is to image the glory of God in the world. We are proposing a similar shift in terms of thinking about the unity of the church. With a verbal inflection, unity becomes more a matter of performance than

---

8. Greggs, *Dogmatic Ecclesiology*, 1:453.
9. For example, McFadyen, "Imaging God."

possession. The key ecclesiological focus needs to shift from how to unite the church to how the church can *perform* the unity and togetherness it desires and image this unity of love and peace and grace to the world. The task of the church is to perform, and so model to others, a way of loving that enables everyone to feel fully alive in God and in the world.

As well as emphasizing the fundamental priority of God in gathering the fragmenting world together in the unity of God, Ephesians also provides practical instruction for how Christians can perform the unity they desire in the midst of ordinary life. In Ephesians 4, Paul recommends a series of essential practices and dispositions to sustain the church in this desire for unity: lowliness, gentleness, patience, and forbearance of one another in love, kindness, tenderheartedness, and forgiveness. Unity is here working from the ground up: through ordinary practices and everyday patterns of behavior that bring people together and sustain the intensity of transformed life. The visible marks of lives lived under God's glory include peace within ourselves, care for others, and love for the beauty of the world and all its inhabitants. And the single most practical imperative suggested in Ephesians is doxological. If there is to be unity, the community should be formed together around a life full of the fullness of prayer: "Pray in the Spirit at all times in every prayer and supplication" (6:18). The fundamental doxological dynamics in Ephesians include blessing (1:1–3), proclamation, praise (1:3, 6, 12, 14), thanksgiving (1:16; 5:4, 20), intercession, singing, psalm reading, and making melody to God (5:20). These doxologies, learned and practiced together, give a picture of what it means for the church to mature fully into the unity it already possesses in God and strives toward.

You could imagine Paul including the prayer in Ephesians 4:1–6 (cited above) as a sort of rhetorical prompt for his readers to pray the petition as their own and as a way of orienting the desires and energies of others to the same end. The prayer is a performative utterance, performing the unity for which the church prays in the hope that the whole world will come to approximate it. The same performative dimension can be seen in Jesus's prayer for unity in John 17, which has inspired so much of the church's working together.[10] The desire of Jesus is above all for a unity of mutual indwelling in love between him, his Father, and those

---

10. See Ford, "Ultimate Desire," and Ford, "Mature Ecumenism's Daring Future."

who respond to them in trust and love. As we listen in on Jesus's deepest desire for unity, we eavesdrop on the intimacy between the Son and the Father being prayed for. Jesus performs in prayer the ultimate unity he desires through his prayer and, by praying, shows to the church what unity looks like: praying, glorifying, and receiving glory so that we too may be "completely one" (17:23). When the church glorifies God in permeations of endless particularity, the church looks beyond the visible things that separate individual churches from each other to the singularity of glory that unites all things in their particularity. Likewise, the very gathering together to say the creed in Christian worship is a performance of the unity the church seeks: it unites Christians across space and time with one another and with the living God. To pray and desire unity together is a form of unity. The *vivens ecclesia* is the church praying together.

If unity is the ultimate desire of the church, it should be the criterion by which to judge when things are wrong. An ever-fractured church, a church defined by what sets communities apart from each other, is a sign of the church lacking in life and fullness, and of desire turned in on itself, blocking rather than channeling the flow of glory in the world. There has always been difference in the life of the church about the most important things possible. There has always been disagreement over how those beliefs are put into practice in the worshiping life of the church. There has always been disagreement over how power and responsibility should be organized and structured. There has always been disagreement over how churches should relate to each other and to other faiths. There has always been disagreement over disagreeing. Glory transforms all this. It transforms difference, with its apparently inevitable tendency to turn disagreement into conflict and competition, into new modes of togetherness, new forms of relationality, and new intimacies in ways that go on stretching minds, hearts, and imaginations.[11] Evading unity, then, is nothing short of evading the glory of God. It is to forget who God is: the glorious One.

On Fullness: Time, Space, and the Saints

The glory of God is the church fully alive together. The church is gathered together by the Spirit to give and receive God's glory in intensive and

11. See again Tonstad, *God and Difference*, 238.

intentional anticipation of the time when all things will glorify God in their entirety and particularity. If glorification has something to do with a change of perception, the church has a particular calling to *see* the world differently—as the theater in which the drama of God's glory unfolds— and to see through things as they are to what they are called to be. As the church is drawn deeper into the world, there can be no manner in which the church can exist for the world without simultaneously receiving from the world something of what the church is called to be.[12] The more the church exists for the world, the more it accompanies the world, the more it joins the world in anticipating the glory that is the chief end of every-thing, and the more it receives from the world something of what that glory can be. The church can be all this—for the world, with the world, and receiving from the world—because the church lives for glory. Signs of the church made alive by the glory of God include the church's unity, holiness, catholicity, and apostolicity. Where there are these marks, there is glory; and where there is glory, there is life. But the glory of God does not stop at bringing the church to life—alive to God, alive to each other, alive to everything—and sustaining the church in the life of God. The glory of God makes the church *fully* alive in every dimension, across every area of church life. In this section we explore more fully the wonder of fullness. What does it mean for the church to be *fully* alive together?

The concept of fullness is a central concern in Ephesians. It can be summed up in the doxological interlude preceding this chapter: the prayer for the church to be "filled with all the fullness [*plērōma*] of God" (3:19). The word *plērōma* is about overflow, fullness beyond completion, unend-ing dynamism.[13] Part of glory's stretching of the imagination is about understanding fullness as more than the state of being full up with no space for more. When it comes to glory, it is never a case of asking "how much is enough" because "the language of enoughness is one of com-petitive economy."[14] The strange, excessive, limitless logic of glory means that the fullness of glory, while completely fulfilling, always has space for more: more abundance, more completion, more glory, and more thirst and hunger for peace and justice to flow in the theater of God's glory. While the overall dynamic in Ephesians is with the riches and fullness

12. On the dynamics of receptivity, see A. Barrett and Harley, *Being Interrupted*.
13. For more on *plērōma*, see Ford, *Self and Salvation*, 107–36.
14. Rogers, *After the Spirit*, 183.

of glorification in the life of the church in the present, the Spirit is still described as the Spirit of promise (1:13). Beyond the riches lavished on the church today, we are marked by the Spirit for the praise of God's glory as a pledge of yet more abundance to come. Other *plērōma* passages in Ephesians include the following:

> With all wisdom and insight he has made known to us the mystery of his will, according to his good pleasure that he set forth in Christ, as a plan for the fullness [*plērōmatos*] of time, to gather up all things in him, things in heaven and things on earth. (Eph. 1:8–10)

> And he has put all things under his feet and has made him the head over all things for the church, which is his body, the fullness [*plērōma*] of him who fills all in all. (Eph. 1:22–23)

And elsewhere in Ephesians, fullness is set alongside the concept of maturity as the church and individuals mature into "the measure of the full [*plērōmatos*] stature of Christ" (4:13).

The idea of the church *fully* alive is explored below in relation to these *plērōma* passages. Following Ephesians, we suggest that one of the most important ways the church can experience the fullness of God's glory is through finding the time (1:9) and the space (1:23) for ever-deepening and intensifying patterns of "togetherness" gathered around the shared glorification of God's glory.

The Fullness of Time

Everything is gathered into the dynamics of glory, including time. When gathered into the life-giving dynamics of glory, time is brought fully to life. As we said in chapter 1, the *Gloria Patri*, sung or spoken in churches around the world today as it has been for centuries, provides an example of glory integrating the three tenses we use to carve up time.

> Glory be to the Father,
> and to the Son,
> and to the Holy Spirit,
> as it was in the beginning,
> is now, and ever shall be, world without end.

Glory does not rest in the past, present, or future alone but exceeds these temporal limitations by bringing each into fullness with one another. Glory is fully a deepening in what has already been given (before the foundation of the world), fully found afresh each day (in ever surprising ways), and fully a stretching into the gradually unfolding gift of unity.

The concern for the "now" of glorification runs strongly through Karl Barth's lectures on Ephesians. In his commentary on Ephesians 1, he says, "A new day has dawned. Yesterday's discovery must be sought anew today. Yesterday's rich are today's poor, and only as the poor will they become rich again. We have not reached the end of the pilgrimage; no goal or stage of an *ordo salutis* has already happened."[15] There is a particular fullness that comes from fully inhabiting the provisional and passing nature of the church present. In the fullness of time, even the best expressions of church life will pass. If "all forms of the church . . . are passing forms," the church is released from fixating on existing patterns of church life and freed into the unfolding of new ecclesial imaginaries resulting from the ongoing formation and re-formation by the excess and surprise of God's glory.[16] Glory integrates the ever-fresh "now" of glorification as a gift of grace "freely bestowed" (Eph. 1:6) and continually "lavished" (1:8) on creation in the present with a deepening into the more of what has already been given. And the past and present tenses of glory are intensified further when fully integrated with the future-oriented, eschatologically stretched yearning for what is "not yet"—of which we have caught glimpses but will come to experience fully in the fullness of time.

The maturing into the triple tense of glory happens over the course of a lifetime and, crucially, in community life as individuals gather together to spend time glorifying God. While communities are shaped in complex, unpredictable, and contextually specific ways, for much of the Christian tradition the most vivifying principle of community life, as we mentioned above, has involved shaping time together around giving praise and glory to God. One of the most profound articulations of a community shaped around the shared glorification of God is Dietrich Bonhoeffer's *Life Together*. While Bonhoeffer did not write much specifically on glory, his chief contribution to the theology of glorification is his practical wisdom

15. Barth, *Epistle to the Ephesians*, 129.
16. Greggs, *Dogmatic Ecclesiology*, 1:452.

on the best ways a community should spend its time growing together into the fullness of glory. The result is a sort of worked-up example of the wisdom of Ephesians 4 on what it takes to sustain community life. While much discussion of the creedal mark of unity is focused on the unity of the whole church (between the world's separated denominations), in both Ephesians and Bonhoeffer there is a massive affirmation of lives lived together on a much more local, everyday level.

The two central chapters of *Life Together* are shaped in particular ways around the temporal conditions of community life. These are the day "together" and the day "alone," both of which are structured around the times of the day. As in Ephesians 6:18, in *Life Together* the single most practical imperative is to spend time together in prayer—alone and with others, shaping the rhythm of the day, week, and year around the rhythms of prayer. From the day's beginning, through midday, and into the evening, at mealtimes, and beyond "set times" for prayer, Bonhoeffer encourages prayer to extend into all time. The "ordering and scheduling of our time will become more secure when it comes from prayer."[17] Perhaps most significantly, Bonhoeffer follows the wisdom of Ephesians 5:19–20 by identifying the psalmody ("the great school of prayer") and the singing of songs as some of the essential doxological practices of community life.[18] And, for Bonhoeffer, the great "secret of the Psalter" is Jesus Christ. The more the community prays the doxologies of the Psalms, the deeper it inhabits the prayer life of Christ and to such a profound extent that Jesus Christ comes to pray "through the mouth of his congregation."[19]

> The Psalter is the prayer book of Jesus Christ in the truest sense of the word. He prayed the Psalter, and now it has become his prayer for all time. . . . Jesus Christ prays the Psalter in his congregation. His congregation prays too, and even the individual prays. But they pray only insofar as Christ prays within them; they pray here not in their own name, but in the name of Jesus Christ. . . . Because Christ prays the prayer of the Psalms with the individual and with the church before the heavenly throne of God, or rather, because those who pray the Psalms are joining in the prayer

17. Bonhoeffer, *Life Together*, 76.
18. Bonhoeffer, *Life Together*, 55.
19. Bonhoeffer, *Life Together*, 54.

of Jesus Christ, their prayer reaches the ears of God. Christ has become their intercessor.[20]

In terms of singing, Bonhoeffer attaches particular significance to singing in unison as a way for Christians to perform the unity they desire.

> It is the voice of the church that is heard in singing together. It is not I who sing, but the church. However, as a member of the church, I may share in its song. Thus all true singing together must serve to widen our spiritual horizon. It must enable us to recognize our small community as a member of the great Christian church on earth and must help us willingly and joyfully to take our place in the song of the church with our singing, be it feeble or good.[21]

Bonhoeffer also recommends other doxologies. There should be time for silence, time for conversation, time for listening, the "special time" to hear the word of God through scriptural meditation, time for eucharistic fellowship, time for action, time for sharing meals together, time for stillness. These doxological practices sustain community life through times of "great inner dryness" and "times of testing," as well as energizing the community to make time for celebration and ultimately for enjoyment of each other's company.[22]

As well as time together, Bonhoeffer is equally interested in the formative importance of spending time alone. Alone as well as together, glory is experienced most fully in the vivifying and daily dynamics of doxologies of various sorts undertaken in solitude and silence—Scripture reading, meditation, prayer, intercession—and, as we will see in the next chapter, is felt most concretely as the experience of joy. We are called not simply to spend time alone but to *enjoy* that time for its own sake. Above all else, for Bonhoeffer, we are called to spend time alone with God enjoying reading Scripture as God's word for us. Here, Bonhoeffer recommends something akin to the form of glory-centered, doxological reading we have been discussing in earlier chapters, which has sustained us in the writing of this book. Indeed, "the most promising way to pray is to allow oneself to

20. Bonhoeffer, *Life Together*, 54–55.
21. Bonhoeffer, *Life Together*, 68.
22. Bonhoeffer, *Life Together*, 88.

be guided by the words of the Bible, to pray on the basis of the words of Scripture."[23] Bonhoeffer suggests slowing down to spend time meditating on individual words and phrases from the Bible.

> It is not necessary that we should get through the entire text in one medita-
> tion. Often we shall have to stick to a single sentence or even to one word
> because we have been gripped and challenged by it and can no longer evade
> it. Are not the words "father," "love," "mercy," "cross," "sanctification," or
> "resurrection" often enough to fill amply the brief period we have set aside
> for our meditation?[24]

Part of the enjoyment that comes from spending time in the sort of medi-tative practice Bonhoeffer recommends is the realization that aloneness and togetherness are mutually intensifying. As Bonhoeffer's reflections on intercessions show, there is no such thing as a truly "solitary" practice of doxology: even alone, we glorify God together.

One of the remarkable features of Bonhoeffer's Ephesians-inflected vision for the formation of life together for the glorification of God is his affirmation of ordinary, everyday life in the present. "Above all," he says, "it is not necessary for us to have any unexpected, extraordinary experiences."[25] This affirmation of the ordinary is true to the dynamics of glory, which claim that small things really matter. Indeed, the glory of God turning up in new, unexpected, everyday places (clouds, burning bushes, the edges of society) has ecclesiological implications for how we understand some of the most practical forms of church life—the late-night committee work; the endless repetition of tea- and coffee-making; opening and closing churches at the beginning and end of the day; the exhausting work of polishing pews, scrubbing floors, sweeping dusty church buildings;[26] the upkeep of graveyards; the maintenance of web-sites and the printing of service sheets; the daily task of praying. In these

---

23. Bonhoeffer, *Life Together*, 89.
24. Bonhoeffer, *Life Together*, 88.
25. Bonhoeffer, *Life Together*, 88.
26. On the holy work of cleaning as an act of "communion, meditation, and belonging," and how much of what is listed above is "usually assigned to women in a society structured through a gendered allocation of responsibility for care, moral integrity, house work, and religious transmission," see the ethnographical study by Abby Day, *The Religious Lives of Older Laywomen*, 74, 103.

local and quotidian activities, glory can be encountered in new ways. In Bonhoeffer, there is nothing particularly radical, nothing much new, no major innovation or novelty, no hot take—just an intensification of tried, tested, and timeless practices that have always energized Christian communities from the beginning even if they have never been immune from danger and damage.[27] Glorification should always be undertaken in the full awareness that some forms of community life, and some of the core practices of those communities, may block the flow of glory in the world. The dynamic of unity too can go terribly and powerfully wrong. What is needed is discernment to identify corruption and perseverance to resist the pressure of any form of unity that does not bring the fullness of life to all.

There remains one further dimension of time worth exploring in relation to the theme of fullness: pace. To experience the fullness of time is not to experience more time at an ever-faster pace. In chapter 1, instead of an orderly, linear movement through variously described fixed stages, we came to understand the *ordo salutis* as expressing something of the "more and more" logic of glory as more of the intensity of God's glory is experienced—more of the "moreness" of God. There is a strange decelerating effect built into the pacing of the *ordo salutis* that makes this deepening into the depths of God's glory unrushable. The *ordo salutis* does not insatiably drive toward quick culmination but recognizes that the possibility of becoming what we are called to be takes time. The stages of the order of salvation (e.g., calling, regeneration, repentance, justification, adoption, sanctification) unfold over time and not necessarily in sequence as Christians pilgrimage into the intensities of glory at a pace set by God, each "stage" both intensifying what has already been given and introducing something even "more," with everything culminating gloriously in glory. There is no shortcut to the glorified end of the Christian life. It is a slow formation that can include leaps and breaks with progression between as well as through each of the stages. The sort of pedagogy being implied here is against, then, the "acceleration of time" that defines so much of ecclesial life in the secular age.[28] As a counter to the "accelerated pushes" of modernity—its speeding up of time for the

---

27. See Cocksworth, "When Prayer Goes Wrong."
28. Root, *The Congregation in a Secular Age*, 59–62.

sake of growth, its preference for the new and innovative, its constant counting and measuring of time in order to squeeze more out of it, and its compulsion to fill time with yet more things to do—when it comes to glorification and its associated practices, there is no rush to the end, no hot pursuit of the next stage, but an encouragement to be patient and gentle (Eph. 4:2) and to deepen into what has already been given, free from the compulsion to skip ahead to the next big thing. This sort of "deceleration" implies a recommitment to the present. Indeed, Barth's somewhat overemphasized "now" of glorification has the benefit of drawing attention to the present, in all its messy realities, rather than longing for an idealized future.

While the world as it is will always be suspicious of the stillness of time, Bonhoeffer reaches deeply into the Christian theological imaginary to think of stillness as "the sign of God's holy presence."[29] The aim is for stillness to "have an impact on the whole day."[30] To experience time fully is about the shaping of time (and indeed space) around simply being together for the sake of being together. Every living thing is made alive together in Christ, who calls us into a radical commitment to each other and a new identity based around enjoying each other and celebrating together for nothing other than the sake of it. In glory, temporality starts to feel different: what matters is the intensity of existence and ever-deepening patterns of "resonance" with others.[31]

What is needed to experience time fully is a combination of the wisdom of the Sabbath and its privileging of resting in the glory of God above everything else (on this, see chap. 4), the sort of patience and gentleness of life instructed in Ephesians, and the disposition of "stillness" recommended by Bonhoeffer in his discussion of time. Also required is the shaping of space to experience time in these ways.

The Fullness of Space

As well as time, space is brought fully to life when gathered into the life-giving dynamics of glory. In one of the key passages found in the

---

29. Bonhoeffer, *Life Together*, 84.

30. Bonhoeffer, *Life Together*, 85.

31. For more on the sociality of "resonance," see Root, *The Congregation in a Secular Age*, 191–213, which offers a theological appropriation of Hartmut Rosa's *Resonance*.

second chapter, Ephesians speaks of the shaping of community life in spatial metaphors:

> In his flesh he has made both groups into one and has broken down the dividing wall, that is, the hostility between us.... In him the whole structure is joined together [*synarmologoumenē*] and grows into a holy temple in the Lord; in whom you also are built together [*synoikodomeisthe*] spiritually into a dwelling place for God. (Eph. 2:14, 21–22)

Notice again those glorious *syn* prefixes conveying the intensity of togetherness. The imagery of a dividing wall in 2:14 probably referred to the wall separating the part of the temple in Jerusalem where only Jews could enter from the part that non-Jews could enter. Once this wall is broken down, space is made fully alive: everyone is brought together in the same space, equally in the presence of the glory of God. When combined with the various sorts of unity mentioned elsewhere in Ephesians, the imagery of the breaking of the wall is a powerful vision of one humanity (2:15) sharing one space, incorporated into one body (2:16; 3:6; 4:4, 25), under one head (1:11), related to one God (4:6), united to God and to each other in one Lord and one baptism (4:5) by the one Spirit (2:18; 4:4) in one faith and one hope (4:4). While Paul probably meant the literal physical barriers that separated Jews from gentiles in the temple, the social imagery can be applied to other barriers in the world today that get in the way of feeling fully alive. The Ephesian dividing wall comes to represent anything that tries to block glory's work of gathering up all things in Christ.

The removal of the barriers in Ephesians 2:14 is not simply about freeing up space or making more of it, just as the fullness of time is not simply about having more time on our hands. What is being imagined is the reshaping of space, the creation of a "holy temple" (2:21). This implies a different structuring of relations, forms of what Willie James Jennings names "sharing" and "communion." In this way, glorification becomes about "the erotic power of God to gather together" and "one that aims to re-create us, reforming us as those who enact gathering and who gesture communion with our very existence."[32] Once the barriers have been

---

32. Jennings, *After Whiteness*, 129, 133, 152.

demolished, those previously on the edges are "brought near" (2:13) and a new social imaginary is formed across past divides.

So long as dividing walls in church and social life remain intact and continue to separate, there is a need to pay particular attention to "the fecundity of 'edge.'"[33] This is the abundance of glory dwelling at or beyond the margins of the life of the church. As we discussed in chapter 1, it is true to the logic of glory to find the light of glory shining especially brightly in these unexpected spaces. Then, on the basis of what is found "at the ends of the world," we are called to cooperate with these findings to interrupt, disrupt, challenge, renew, transform, and intensify the mission and ministry of the church.[34]

In terms of the unity of the church, the challenge is for the dividing walls that separate Christian communities to fall in such a way that enables new forms of togetherness and peaceable diversity without reproducing further division and violence. In this new, utterly inclusive space, there is space for everyone: "all the saints" (Eph. 1:15), "every spiritual blessing" (1:3), "all wisdom and insight" (1:8), and much more. Yet within this abundant capaciousness, there is no space for coercive and competitive malformations of community life (4:25–31). What fills this space instead is an ethic of "gentleness, with patience, bearing with one another in love" (4:2) and being "kind to one another, tenderhearted, forgiving one another" (4:32).

The reference to singing and making music in Ephesians (5:19) can help us imagine the sort of fullness that is beyond competition. Think of the way two notes can fill the same space without a sense of overcrowding or canceling each other out. It does not make sense to think of one note needing to cede the other space to sound. Instead, they are enhanced together as they "resonate" with each other and bring each into further fullness when gathered into deeper harmony—they make each other fully alive.[35] Sound surrounds us, engulfs us, goes right through us, *overwhelms*

---

33. A. Barrett, *Interrupting the Church's Flow*, 179–81. As Barrett argues, this has an impact on the way the church shapes its worship. For a community whose focus is being gathered together in Christ, the shape of Christian liturgy tends to put emphasis on the "sending" of the community out into the world. What would it mean for churches to "reverse the flow" of the liturgy so that it provides space for the community to be as well gathered as it is sent? And what would these doxological practices of gathering look like?

34. On this, see Carvalhaes, *Liturgies from Below*.

35. See Begbie, "Through Music," and Ford, *Self and Salvation*, 135.

us in such a way that does not overcome us and, indeed, in such a way that combines the temporal tenses. The three types of singing mentioned in Ephesians include psalms (the songs of the past), hymns (the songs of the present), and spiritual songs (the songs of the Spirit that improvise on both past and present to anticipate something of future glory).

In her critique of patterns of theological reflection that render "good relations between persons (divine or human)" dependent on "making room for another," Linn Tonstad offers another way of imagining space that does not depend on the need to "move aside to make room for the other, for there is enough space for all."[36] The imagery of "banquets without borders" in Tonstad's discussion of glory comes to express new possibilities of life, new intimacies, new performances of togetherness: "One spatial way to represent the character of this transformation is to imagine the heavenly banquet table around which we gather as simultaneously huge and tiny—everyone crowds in next to each other, yet somehow, the closer everyone gets, there is always room for all."[37] In the feasts of holy banquets, we learn that we do not need to get out of the way for others to flourish, but we can enjoy together the overflow of abundance that characterizes the life of glory given by God, free from the boundaries, borders, and walls that otherwise divide us and shape space competitively. What better vision is there of the fullness of glory than taking full delight in each other's company, lives, and experiences, and being drawn deeper together through an ethic of kindness, gentleness, patience, compassion, and forgiveness in the feasting, celebrating, and delighting for the sake of others?

Essential to glorification is deep and holy immersion in life together. The saints, in Ephesians (3:18), are those who have matured fully in Christ and inhabited most fully the fullness of time and space to find, give, and receive God's glory together. The "community of saints," which is mentioned in the Apostles' Creed but not in the Nicene Creed, reminds the church of its geographical (space) and temporal (time) extensities. The saints remind the church that it stretches, as glory stretches, beyond the spatiotemporal conditions of the present—across time, geographical distance, national borders and cultures, age, ethnicity, sexuality, gender, class, and congregational and denominational dividing walls separating

36. Tonstad, *God and Difference*, 13, 239.
37. Tonstad, *God and Difference*, 243.

the church from itself. The saints remind us that we live under a holy
canopy that offers an identity larger than ourselves by holding us in kinship with an unending community, uniting those who have come before
and those who will go after us with the present, and embracing those
through the centuries and around the world today who glorify God with
all their hearts, minds, souls, and strength.

Working toward Unity

For the church to live a life worthy of its calling, it needs to be committed
to practical ways of working together toward durable models of unity.
Receptive Ecumenism is a practical way for churches to work together
and has helped reenergize the ecumenical movement with a bold vision
for church unity. While we have drawn from Ephesians and Bonhoeffer
the importance of local, everyday forms of unity, Receptive Ecumenism
works on a much grander scale. Daring a vision for church unity beyond
spiritual, practical, and local forms of ecumenism, Receptive Ecumenism
aims "towards full structural, ministerial, sacramental communion" of a
currently divided church.[38] It works toward the full unity of the church
across every area of ecclesial life by approaching the points of difference
between different traditions as gifts to be received rather than obstacles
to overcome. As Paul D. Murray explains,

> Receptive Ecumenism represents a remarkably simple but far-reaching
> strategy that seeks to draw out a value that has been at work, to some de
> gree at least, in all good ecumenical encounter and to place it centre-stage
> now as the appropriate organizing principle for contemporary ecumenism.
> This is the principle that considerable further progress is indeed possible,
> but only if each of the traditions, both singly and jointly, makes a clear,
> programmatic shift from prioritizing the question "What do our various
> others first need to learn from us?" to asking instead, "What is it that *we*
> need to learn and can learn, or receive, with integrity from others?"[39]

Every church should be asking the core Receptive Ecumenism question in
respect of glorification: What is it that *we* need to receive with integrity

---

38. Murray, "Introducing Receptive Ecumenism," 7.
39. Murray, "Introducing Receptive Ecumenism," 1.

from other church traditions about the glorification of God? For individual churches to be fully alive, they must be open to the widest range of doxological interruptions from beyond their own borders.

It would be a fascinating exercise in Receptive Ecumenism to bring different theological understandings of glorification into mutually intensifying conversations of ecclesial learning. What can Karl Barth's densely theocentric theology of the perfection of glory learn from Mayra Rivera's concern for the damage that has been inflicted in the name of God's glory in the history of colonialism? What can Hans Urs von Balthasar's account of the aesthetics of glory learn from Jonathan Edwards's attention to the affective shape of glorification? It would be more fascinating still to shift the learning from particular theologians to the diversity of doxological practice flowing through the traditions of the church, on the vivacious edges of ecclesial life, and beyond the borders of the church to inspire shared learning around doxological practice. When it comes to glorification, the possibilities for ecclesial learning are endless.

A significant body of literature has emerged around the theological, philosophical, and affective themes in Receptive Ecumenism and especially in terms of its core dynamic of gift reception.[40] While its biblical features are also gaining attention, there has not been as much work to bring to the surface its spiritual shape.[41] Gabrielle Thomas's fascinating use of Receptive Ecumenism to explore women's experiences of working together in churches in England is an exception.[42] Thomas shows that prayer is "a core aspect of the receptive journey."[43] What would it mean to understand Receptive Ecumenism not only as involving prayer along the way to unity or leading to the embrace of prayer (as in spiritual ecumenism), but as a form of prayer itself, a sort of doxology, a way of praising God and performing togetherness? Like glorification, the dynamic of Receptive Ecumenism involves more than the highest possible tolerance for multiple opinions. It is concerned with the deep sociality—the *synergy*—that comes from learning from difference. There is something, therefore, in the dynamic of receptivity itself, in addition to the actual gifts received, that is a sign of the church fully alive—a sign of the church

40. See Murray, Ryan, and Lakeland, *Receptive Ecumenism as Ecclesial Learning*.
41. See Pizzey, *Receptive Ecumenism*, 135.
42. Thomas, *For the Good of the Church*.
43. Thomas, *For the Good of the Church*, 42.

willing and eager to journey together into the unity it desires. Thus, Receptive Ecumenism embraces the full ethic of doxological togetherness described in Ephesians 4: humility, gentleness, bearing with each other in love (4:2), kindness, compassion, and forgiveness (4:32). Especially relevant to the whole ecumenical enterprise is patience (4:1). Working toward the unity of the church is a messy, complicated, relational process that matures in the fullness of time.

The main encouragement of this chapter is to enter more fully the dynamics of glory by discovering the abundance of glory in different expressions of church life, and then to allow these doxological discoveries to flow back into the life of your own church, intensifying what is already there. Part of a formation in glory, then, involves becoming maximally receptive to the diversity of glorification at play in the theater of glory: to notice it, describe it, learn from it; to be "sentinels," as the Anglican ordinal sometimes has it, watching for the signs of God's glory in the church and beyond, including keeping watch—day and night—for glory's distortions.

Every church needs to be fully alive to the first doxological languages of those beyond the boundaries of its own life. To adapt something Jennings says of learning another's native language, learning another's doxological vernacular means coming "to love the people—the food, the faces, the plans, the practices, the songs, the poetry, the happiness, the sadness, the ambiguity, the truth," and "their land, their landscapes, their home."[44] It means deep intimacies and patterns of togetherness.

If there is one church tradition known for an especially glorious mother tongue, that tradition is Pentecostalism. The deep inhabitation of the Spirit of glory embodied in Pentecostal experience can inspire in other traditions new patterns of doxological activity and the renewal of existing patterns. In his extraordinary analysis of the "plenitudinous folds" of "Blackpentecostal doxology," Ashon T. Crawley explores whooping, shouting (which is dance), glossolalia, and tarrying in the Spirit as examples of what he calls doxological "breath."[45] Each "is fundamentally about

---

44. Jennings, *Acts*, 30.

45. Crawley, *Blackpentecostal Breath*. Written (or, better, composed and performed) by a sometime preacher, choir director, and organist in the Church of God in Christ, a large Black Pentecostal denomination, *Blackpentecostal Breath* sits on the interdisciplinary "nexus of performance theory, queer theory, sound studies, literary theory, theological studies, and continental theology." The book is too far-reaching and with too much significance

having being-together as an irreducible plurality, irreducible density."[46] These practices are fully sensual, affective, embodied, material, kinetic, sonic, and visual—and yet have long legacies of ecclesial suppression.[47] Tarrying is particularly relevant to our discussion. Tarrying means "waiting with fervent prayer and song—intensely for the experience of Spirit baptism."[48] It is a practice of anticipation and discloses a theology of expectation as the church calls for more of God's grace, further revelation of what has already been given, and deeper intensification of the known unknown of God's glory. Imagine not simply confessing the marks of the church in a creed but tarrying for them as intensively as you might wait in prayer and song for more of God's glory.

Doxological sound, like glory itself, breathes the air of excess. Whooping (the moment of celebration when the "sermon is unleashed") is ultimately "an excessive otherwise of breath."[49] It signifies the freedom to breathe not only freely but also extravagantly and without resistance or policing. Crawley finds, then, in the choreography of these doxologies a "mode of being together that is the condition of occasion for envisioning, and living into such envisioning, a critique of the known—the violent, oppressive, normative—world."[50] The performance "of sharing, of being together tightly in space and moving together," based on "radical openness and sociality," inspires for Crawley a different sort of world, perhaps too a different sort of church.

Ecumenical engagement tends to work with what is already there. Receptive Ecumenism, for example, seeks to create the conditions for the better flow of the gifts already present in the life of individual churches to be received by other churches in a move toward greater levels of unity. Spiritual ecumenism works with the shared givens of the liturgical lives of different churches to find better ways of celebrating what is doxologically already there.[51] Practical forms of ecumenical action seek better working relations among churches around existing shared concerns to transform

---

to summarize adequately here, but it can be pushed in theological directions Crawley does not explicitly travel.

46. Crawley, *Blackpentecostal Breath*, 237.
47. See C. Sanders, *Saints in Exile*.
48. Crawley, *Blackpentecostal Breath*, 10.
49. Crawley, *Blackpentecostal Breath*, 46.
50. Crawley, *Blackpentecostal Breath*, 4.
51. See Kasper, *Handbook of Spiritual Ecumenism*.

the given present into a more just future. Indeed, it has become the cus-
tomary instinct in much of contemporary Protestant theology to look
to the givens in ecclesial life and practice or to the church's past for the
wisdom needed to heal the damage of the present. However, taking cues
from Crawley, what would it mean to push the limits of ecclesial imagination beyond receiving or recovering what is already "there" in order to
inhabit the possibility of "otherwise"—a desire beyond "what is and has
been given"?[52] Perhaps the main gift to be received from the doxological
aesthetics Crawley discusses in *Blackpentecostal Breath* is not ever more
diverse ways of glorifying God but a new ecclesial imaginary. Put differently, and in terms of the moods of faith, "otherwise" shifts the mood of
the marks of the creed from the optative (desiring the future unity of the
church awaiting us) to the subjunctive (embracing the possibility of the
"what if").

We are called by Ephesians toward something "abundantly far more
than all we can ask or imagine" (3:20), yet we move toward this known
unknown end joyfully, trusting the God of surprises. There are no facts
about the future. We can act into the future and desire a future good, but
we cannot work backward from a vision we have set in advance. Nowhere
in Ephesians or elsewhere is there an answer to the question of what the
unity of the church will actually look like. There is no detailed definition
or fixed blueprint. The church's stretching into the fullness of unity is a
"mystery of the gospel" (6:19), an end to which we are called and which
we trust wholeheartedly but do not understand. Gregory of Nyssa knew
this dynamic as *epektasis*—the inexhaustible stretching of desire, mind,
imagination, heart, and action into the superabundant knowledge, love,
and glory of God.[53] Perhaps that is what the best doxological practice
prepares the church for: a stretching toward a surprise-filled future that
it does not yet know and cannot control. We can tarry for unity, we can
actively pursue it and work toward the conditions for its future possibility, but the unity to which the church is called is itself a calling—it is an
invocation of God.

In this chapter on the ecclesiology of glory, we have said that the church
is most fully alive when fully alive together. When the church gathers

---

52. Crawley, *Blackpentecostal Breath*, 2.
53. Gregory of Nyssa, *Life of Moses*, 30. See also Thomas, "The Cappadocians on the
Beauty and Efficacy of Prayer."

together for the glorification of God, it experiences the fullness of life in time and space as witnessed by those who have matured fully in glory—the communion of saints. Journeying into life together, and all the fullness of life such an existence implies, requires the formation in trust offered by the Nicene Creed, the wisdom of Ephesians and its attention to everyday practices, the ambition of Receptive Ecumenism and its daring desire for full unity across every area of ecclesial life, and the energy of the forms of doxological life Crawley expresses through the concept of "otherwise." In the next chapter we turn from life together to the life of individuals to explore more of what it might mean to be glorified in the life of the church. What account of the Christian life emerges from the ecclesial spirituality discussed in this chapter? How can you experience the glorious unity of God? What does it mean to embody that glory in the world today? And how is glorification enacted in the world to make earth as well as heaven fully resplendent with God's glory?

DOXOLOGICAL INTERLUDE

Psalm 145

¹ *A praising, for David.*[1]

Alef   I exalt You, my God, the King; let me bless Your name forever and ever.

² *Bet*   Every day I bless You; let me praise Your name forever and ever.

³ *Gimel*   Great is Adonai[2] and highly praiseworthy; there is no exhausting His greatness.

⁴ *Dalet*   Generation to generation extols Your works, and Your mighty acts they declare.

⁵ *He*   The glorious splendor of Your majesty and Your marvelous deeds I ponder.

⁶ *Vav*   The power of Your awesome acts they tell, and Your greatness I recount.

1. We are using Ellen Davis's translation, which will appear in the forthcoming *The Chapel Hymnal*, ed. Zebulon Highben (St. Louis: ECS Publishing Group). Psalm 145 (144 LXX) is an alphabetic poem. Each of twenty-one of the twenty-two letters of the Hebrew alphabet begins each of its twenty-one verses, and the Septuagint and other ancient versions give us the missing verse 13a. Davis writes,

> The alphabetic form implies completeness; this is total praise, from *aleph* to *tav*—in effect, from A to Z—and still "there is no exhausting [God's] greatness" (v. 3). The alphabet was a West Semitic invention of the second millennium BCE, which through the centuries spread around the Mediterranean Rim in slightly variant forms. It was a world-shaping discovery, and some Israelite poets evidently reveled in it, adapting their own creativity to reflect its genius. (Davis, Fujimura, and Held, *Light within Light* [forthcoming])

2. Adonai is a traditional pronunciation for YHWH, the (deliberately, in Jewish practice) "unpronounceable name of God."

7	*Zayin*	They celebrate Your lavish goodness, and of Your righteousness they sing.
8	*Ḥet*	Gracious and merciful is ADONAI, long in patience and great in covenant-love.
9	*Tet*	Good is ADONAI to all, and His compassion is upon all His works.
10	*Yod*	All Your works acclaim You, O ADONAI, and those true to You bless You!
11	*Kaf*	The glory of Your sovereignty they tell, and of Your might they speak,
12	*Lamed*	to make known to the human family Your might, and the glorious splendor of Your sovereignty.
13	*Mem*	Your sovereignty is sovereignty through all ages, and Your governance in every single generation.
13a	*Nun*	Faithful is ADONAI in all His words and covenant-committed in all His works.
14	*Samekh*	ADONAI is supporting all who are fallen and raising up all who have collapsed.
15	*Ayin*	The eyes of all look eagerly to You, as You give them their food in its season,
16	*Peh*	opening Your hand, and fully satisfying the right-desire of all who live.
17	*Tsadi*	Righteous is ADONAI in all His ways and covenant-true in all His doings.
18	*Qof*	Close is ADONAI to all who call upon Him, to all who call on Him in truth.
19	*Resh*	The desire of those who fear Him He meets; their cry He hears, and He delivers them.
20	*Shin*	ADONAI watches over all who love Him, but all the wicked He brings to naught.
21	*Tav*	The praise of ADONAI my mouth utters; let all flesh bless His holy Name forevermore.

CHAPTER FOUR

The Christian Life and Glorification

FROM THE RADIANT GLORY of the divine life of God, through some of the seminal glory texts in the Bible, to the church brought fully alive together by the glory of God, and now to the Christian life, we have traveled some way in this short book. In this final chapter, we circle back to the dynamics of glory first articulated in the introduction to ask, What does it mean to be attracted into the glory of God? We focus on three aspects of being glorified by God: glory experienced (as joy), glory embodied (in the smile), and glory enacted (in Sabbath rest, blessing, and glorifying). Throughout, we once again take Irenaeus's claim that the glory of God is a human being "fully alive" as our guiding principle, which we expand and intensify as we move through the chapter.

Experiencing Glory

A doxological anthropology gathers everything—the somatic, moral, aesthetic, intellectual, emotional, spiritual, ecological—together into a dynamic of mutual intensification. The glory of God is felt in the friction that comes from rubbing the fragments of the fractured self together, as well as in the fragments themselves. Because of this interconnectedness,

it is difficult to think about glorification apart from the tangible experiences of glory in the Christian life.[1] In fact, it is difficult to *think* about
glory altogether. Thinking about glory is like painting a bird in flight or
wording a radiance. Glory is a feeling more than an idea. It is no wonder,
then, that some of the greatest theorizers of glory have come at glory
via the affections. Jonathan Edwards, Hans Urs von Balthasar, and even
those more distrustful of the category of experience, such as Karl Barth,
have looked to the affections to find the right language to speak of glory.

Since glory's "power of attraction" concerns all things, the range of
emotions implicated by glory is gloriously broad.[2] The most appropriate
affections corresponding to glory include astonishment, surprise, wonder,
even terror and fear. Theology is and should be nothing short of terrifying, especially when it gets close to the most hallowed ground of God's
glory—and if not terrifying, certainly ambiguous. Glory is a discourse
that defies easy definition, and the experience of glory is the experience of
something of the ambiguity of the human condition under God. So the
glory of God resides "in the cloud" (Exod. 16:10), a "cloud of unknow-
ing," as the unnamed English mystic put it. However, glorification is not
just about bringing things to their chief end; rather, through glory everything is renewed in light of that end. Every dimension of life is caught up
in the transformative dynamics of glory, including theology itself. The
words we use to speak of God are drawn through fear and trembling into
the hope of doing better descriptive justice to the experience of God's
unfathomable holiness. The constant surprise of doxological theology is
that the words we use to speak of a theme even as impossibly strange as
glory hold the possibility of conveying fragments of that truth as they are
brought into fullness—that is, sanctified—by glory. Where there is talk of
God's glory, feelings of astonishment and surprise are never far away. Also
surprising, as we have said, is glory's habit of turning up in unexpected
places, upturning prior conceptions of what we initially thought it to be.
As Kristine A. Culp writes, "God is always forming and re-forming the

---

1. As Simeon Zahl argues in *The Holy Spirit and Christian Experience*, theological engagement with the category of experience is inescapable for the theologian. We follow Zahl's
argument in this chapter on several counts: the inescapability of experience, doctrines have
"affective salience," experience is "practically recognisable" in the Christian life, speaking of
experience means attending to the ordinary, and experience is a pneumatological concept.

2. Barth, *CD* II/1, 650.

mundane, vulnerable stuff of creaturely existence, breathing life and glory into it."[3] The great surprise is that glory can be found in and through the brokenness of the world, as it is found in and through the broken body of Christ.

What about wonder? For Mayra Rivera, "glory is the event that lures us into the experience of wonder."[4] Christian living is as much about wondering why the world falls short of God's glory as being lost in wonder, love, and praise. Wonder continually questions, explores, and interrogates the way things are; and this wondering tips over into longing.[5] There is a restless impulse built into the dynamics of glory that leaves us, like Moses, always longing for more: longing to encounter more of the divine life; longing to see God face to face; longing to desire more of the things God desires; longing to be changed from one degree of glory to another; longing for more of "the glory . . . to be revealed to us" (Rom. 8:18); longing for more intensive relations of belonging; longing for a world beyond despair; longing for our desires to be intensified by the longings of the Lord's Prayer—for the kingdom to come, for God's will to be done, for the end of hunger, for peace—and stretched further by the ultimate longings of Jesus's prayer in John 17 that we may be completely one with God, as the Father and the Son are one.

When it comes to thinking affectively about glory, the famous Westminster Catechisms do not lead with wonder, astonishment, or longing. The chief end awaiting humanity does not stop with the glorification of God, nor does it stop with simply seeing glory at work in the world. In the theater of glory, God's creatures are not merely spectators but join "with" glory by experiencing glory in the midst of their lives. To cite Edwards, "God is glorified not only by His glory's being seen, but by its being rejoiced in."[6] And as Barth says, "Glory . . . awakens joy, and is itself joyful."[7] Even more than glorifying God, the Westminster Catechisms show, then, that humanity's ultimate calling is to enjoy God and—moreover—to enjoy God forever. The natural pairing to glory is joy, the most doxological emotion. The glorified life is one of joy, rejoicing, and enjoyment as we

3. Culp, *Vulnerability and Glory*, 94.
4. Rivera, "Glory," 168.
5. See Southgate, *Theology in a Suffering World*.
6. Edwards, *Works of Jonathan Edwards*, 13:495.
7. Barth, *CD* II/1, 655.

are enjoined in the joy of God. Calvin hints at this: If the world is the theater of God's glory, the world is a place of play, bringing joy to hearts and putting smiles on faces. Joy is what makes everything worthwhile.

It is right, then, that the canticle following the Benedicite in the Morning Prayer liturgy of the Anglican Office is the *Jubilate Deo*, which begins,

> O be joyful in the Lord,
> all ye lands: serve the Lord with gladness,
> and come before his presence with a song.

As we are attracted deeper into the glory of the divine life and further into the radiance of that glory in the world, God's glory rests on bodies as feelings of joy. All things, and all things in their particularity, feel something of this joy. The sun, the pastures, and the meadows act and sing with joy (Pss. 19:4–5; 65:12–13); the mountains, the hills, and the trees of the field—all the land is filled with joy and serves God joyfully (Isa. 55:12). Moreover, as all created things rejoice in their particularity, joy is gathered up together in Christ to cohere in mutually intensifying, vivifying dances. Joy is what makes us feel the fullness of life together. And the life of glorification involves working together to curate spaces full of joy and to remove obstacles that block the flow of joy in the world. Joy is deeply personal and utterly social, and best experienced together.

Insofar as theology is doxological, theology is joyful. As Barth says, dogmatics is a "singularly beautiful and joyful science, so that it is only willingly and cheerfully that we can be theologians."[8] When involved in the formal tasks of theology, you can get lost in the business of reading articles, writing books, teaching courses, preparing sermons, interpreting dense passages of scholarly argument. Every so often it is worth pausing to take stock of the wonder of being able to speak of a mystery so mysterious as the glory of God and the endless joy that comes from such an endeavor. Without joy the theologian would take themselves too seriously, whereas

8. Barth, *CD* IV/3.2, 881. His revisionist doctrine of election at least in part was motivated by the worry that the doctrine of predestination classically understood in his own Reformed tradition did not elicit sufficient joy, whereas for Barth election is surely the most joyous of all doctrines. It must "awaken only joy, pure joy" (*CD* II/2, 174). See Starkenburg, "No Cowering Down." For a genealogy of "grim theologians" and of those who break the mold, such as Barth, see Berger, *Redeeming Laughter*, 183–89.

joy acknowledges the finitude and provisionality of the task in hand. Being released from the burden of having to say everything liberates us to find joy in what can be said and to enjoy theology for its own sake.

In the first of several expansions of the Irenaean aphorism that has guided this book from the start, we suggest in this first section that the glory of God is even more than being fully alive: it is about being "joy-fully alive." Here, we follow Rubem Alves's improvisation on Irenaeus in his theo-poetics of the body, where he writes, "The glory of God is found in happy people," which we explore through the themes of abundance and "respair."[9]

Abundant Joy

Like glorification, joy often gets filed at the eschatological end of things. It speaks of the final destination, the chief end to which all of creation is called, which is a homecoming, a returning to that from which we were created. It is the chief vocation of all things and the supreme mark of the consummation of life with God. It gives us something to hope for and something to guide our energies toward. The Christian life needs these coordinates. However, as much as joy is the "last thing," it is also the ultimate calling today. And if we really are to rejoice always, as Paul says we should (Phil. 4:4), joy needs to be understood in terms of the everyday, in the daily decision to find joy in the ordinary. As with glory, there is a "found" dimension to joy. You can give joy to others, you can receive joy from others too, but joy concentrates attention on the glimpses of glory in the unpredictable ordinariness of life as well as those peak experiences that leave us jumping for joy.[10]

Whenever and however we experience joy, we experience the abundance of God. On a basic level, joy is abundant in meaning (2 Cor. 8:2). Everything we said about fullness (*plērōma*) in chapter 3 applies here too, as the psalmist says:

> In your presence there is fullness of joy;
> in your right hand are pleasures forevermore. (Ps. 15:11 LXX
> [16:11 Eng.])

---

9. Alves, *I Believe in the Resurrection of the Body*, 20, cited in Rivera, "Glory," 167. *Respair* is an old word, fallen out of usage, that is derived from the Latin *re* (back) and *sperare* (to hope).
10. Mathewes, "Some Remarks on Joy," 96.

In the Septuagint, "joy" is *euphrosynēs*—which gets at something of the euphoria of joy. This euphoria is indescribable, "unspeakable," and infinitely capacious.[11] We can be aware of joy when we feel it rushing through our bodies and surging through our flesh, and when we encounter it enlivening the lives of others, but the deep things of joy, like love and peace, are difficult to describe. We know when it is there and feel its absence, but putting joy into words seems to undersell it, never matching the fullness of the experience itself. Part of the Christian life, then, is about living in the uncertainty of being called to bear the fruit of something we cannot with any certainty say we fully understand. It is another known unknown. Or, better, part of the joy of joy is about letting joy be joy without having to explain it. We are called to enjoy God for God's sake rather than what can be gained from it, which in turn presses us to enjoy creation for creation's sake and then others for their own sake without strings attached. When so much of life comes down to means-end transactions, joy expands life for extravagant, endless generosity.

Primarily, joy is abundant in meaning because it has its source in the abundance of God. Joy flows abundantly in the divine life of God as the Father and the Son in the Holy Spirit share in the joy that makes them complete. As well as moving energetically and excessively within the divine life of God, glory radiates from God as joy, effulgently and lavishly filling the world with the resplendent gladness that gives all things strength and fullness. The glory of God leaves its mark, like a seal imprinting hot wax, on bodies as joy. "God's glory is the indwelling joy of His divine being which as such shines out from Him, which overflows in its richness, which in its super-abundance is not satisfied with itself but communicates itself."[12] Then joy circles back to God as God finds enjoyment in all things being joy-fully alive. The more we rejoice in God, the more God rejoices in our enjoyment, and the more joy radiates from the life of God in ever more intensifying waves of mutual enjoyment. To take joy in something, therefore, is to take something of God and to have that gift energize and direct our being and acting in the world. Christ prays "that my joy may be in you, and that your joy may be full" (John 15:11).

In another sense, joy is abundant because it is concerned with excess. Often in the New Testament, the word *joy* is qualified by superlatives that

---

11. See Holmes, *Joy Unspeakable.*
12. Barth, *CD* II/1, 647.

push joy beyond the limits of language. Think of the *"great* joy" of the news of the birth of Christ in Luke 2:10 and again in Luke 24:52 when the disciples return to Jerusalem after the ascension of Christ. Think of when John the Baptist is said to "rejoice *exceedingly"* at the news of Jesus's conception, even while he is still in the womb (Luke 1:41–44). Likewise, when the magi see the star as a sign of the birth of Christ, they "rejoiced *exceedingly* with *great* joy" (Matt. 2:10 RSV). Think, ultimately, of the *"glorious* joy [*dedoxasmenē*]" in 1 Peter 1:8. This wonderfully dense Greek word means something like the inexpressible joy that has been glorified. Even joy is made fully alive by the dynamics of glory as it gets glorified by glory.

We are building a picture of joy as more than what comes from having basic needs met. It is more than being full to the brim. It goes beyond the bare minimum and the strictly necessary. The fullness of joy is a fullness that reaches beyond being "filled up," even filled with no room for more. It is always greater, still "more excellent," as Calvin says of glorification.[13] Just as the dynamics of glory are infinitely energetic—radiating and attracting in a movement of call and response that leads to still more intensified forms of relationality on every level—the experience of this dynamic is the unceasing, bottomless, superabundant, euphoric joy in God. Unendingly climaxing, glorious joy is the dance that never ends, the crescendo that keeps building, the music that does not fade, the narrative that keeps culminating, the holy banquet with yet more courses and more space for more.

By "joy," then, we mean the fullest possible flourishing.[14] "Joy awakens all our senses, energizing mind and body," and in such a way that does not override but intensifies other experiences of God's glory.[15] The more we experience joy, the more we love, the more we are astonished, the more we long, and the more those around us experience joy in their lives as all things are drawn into joy's dialectic of mutual enjoyment. Joy intensifies

13. Calvin, *The Epistles of Paul*, 157.
14. There is wonderful symmetry built into Barth's dogmatic handling of joy. His first principal treatment of joy takes place in the context of his doctrine of glory in *CD* II/1, under the theme "The Perfections of Divine Freedom"; the second, this time within the ethics of creation in *CD* III/4, takes place under the theme "The Freedom for Life." In both, joy speaks of that which increases and intensifies our fundamental capacities for freedom.
15. Moltmann, "Christianity: A Religion of Joy," 2.

a sense of longing too and even struggle as one is energized to cultivate ever-richer practices of engagement with God, the world, others, and the self—each for their own sakes. And most critically, from joy flows an ethic of resistance against despair.

Respairing Joy

The cries of despair weigh heavily on any account of the Christian life, especially one that puts joy at its heart and end. As Rivera says, "A theology of glory that seeks to be meaningful in the midst of concrete realities of injustice and pain cannot ignore the horrors with which it is associated."[16] It may even feel scandalous to cultivate lives full of joy when so much in the world blocks joy and gets in the way of feeling fully alive. Should we really advocate joy when creation is groaning so loudly in pain? Surely, grief, sorrow, or even despair would be more appropriate. How might our doxological practice need to respond to a new situation, in which many of us are flooded with news from around the world, much of it bad news, and there are repeated warnings of potential disasters? Does the Christian life need to inhabit more fully doxologies in the minor key? The church is in urgent need of new scripts for these times of trauma, ones that allow space for loss and despair without resolving everything too quickly into the narrative of hope and joy.[17]

There is an important need, then, to distinguish the joy we are talking about from the oppressive joy that assumes "nothing is really pathological, damaging or painful."[18] In everyday life, the way we talk about joy, and the pressure to be joyful, can sometimes give this impression. Likewise, the way Barth speaks of "anticipatory joy" could be seen to displace attention from the difficulties of existing in the present to some anticipated future full of joy and free from despair.[19] Any account of the Christian life that relentlessly skips over the way things are in the rush to feel fully alive, or presumes to make joy seem easy in the midst of the unpredictability

16. Rivera, "Glory," 175.
17. There are some connections here to trauma theology's deferral of hope. See Rambo, *Spirit and Trauma*, and O'Donnell, *Broken Bodies*. For a more developed account of the practices we have in mind, see O'Donnell's forthcoming *Survival: Radical Spiritual Practices for Trauma Survivors*.
18. McFadyen, *Bound to Sin*, 211.
19. Barth, *CD* III/4, 377.

of life, is too minimal in comparison with the joy that has its origins in divine glory.

The joy emerging from the deep reflexes of the dynamics of glory can be termed "respairing joy." Whereas to *despair* suggests a loss of hope, the old English word *respair* refers to a sense of hope in the midst of a despairing world. Indeed, as the light of God's glory radiates, the sources of despair are illumined for all to see. The more we experience God's glorious joy, and the brighter that glory shines in the world, the more alert we become to the multiple ways the world falls short of the glory of God. There is an epistemological dimension to joy that follows a similar logic to Barth's insight that sin is so intoxicating that we need the sobering revelation of God in Jesus Christ by the Spirit to understand the depths of disorder for ourselves.[20] Only from the perspective of being glorified by God, Barth would say, can the full extent of the agonizing joylessness of evil be known. Or, put positively, because God is a God of joy, you can see reality for what it is only when you see the world through joy rather than despair. When hope cannot be felt and radical disappointment approaches complete despair, joy pulls us back into trusting that the only ultimate is the enjoyment that marks the life of glorification.

Respairing joy, as a practice of re-hoping, avoids the presumption of triumphalism that covers up the cries of despair with the sounds of joy. Such triumphalism is not available to the joy that is derived from the glory of God because this joy cannot be understood apart from the full history of the life, death, and resurrection of Jesus Christ. When we are called to "rejoice always," it is not that we are called to find joy where joy cannot be found but that when we have joy, we have joy "in the Lord" (Phil. 4:4). Implied in the idea of "joy in the Lord" is the full story of Jesus Christ as narrated by the Nicene Creed: birth, death, and resurrection. As such, the Nicene Creed compels us to think of joy in the context of the cross. Alistair McFadyen writes, "Joy that has gone through the cross must allow the crosses of the world to stand, just as the resurrection allowed Jesus' cross to stand, worked through and with the pathological dynamics to reorient them and to draw the damage into relation to the abundance and fullness of God."[21] In every experience of joy there remains a fragment

20. Barth, *CD* IV/1, 361.
21. McFadyen, *Bound to Sin*, 211.

of the cross that still stands. This makes the cry of despair, as Rivera says, "not the negation of glory, but the negation of its negation. The cry of a hungry person and the groaning of creation manifest the persistence of glory, the astonishing fact that all the world's callousness and violence have not overcome it."[22] If the resurrection is the claim that there is something more to life than despair, joy is the experience of this something more.

To invite joy is not to sidestep despair. Instead, joy addresses the numbing effect despair has on life that makes a way out of the way things are feel unimaginable. Joy overcomes the failure to imagine there is no alternative, no "otherwise." It disciplines the body to re-hope against despair by filling bodies with tangible experiences of the resurrection promise that everything will be alright in the end; and if it is not alright, it is not the end, for we know (that is, our *bodies* know) the chief end is joy in all its glory. The Spirit, the giver of life, who bears in us a feeling of a better future, charges the body for more of that future in the present and calls each of us into a dialectic of rejoicing and respairing.

Here Christian theology has something of real importance to say to the world. It calls into question the rituals of late-modern selfhood that are increasingly geared toward a "minimally positive outlook on life."[23] These rituals combine to feed the imagination with yet more reasons to lose hope—doomscrolling, the specter of negative bias in the twenty-four-hour news cycle, the loss of trust in the institutions that care for us, the breakdown of community life that sustains social spaces for joy. The pedagogy of joy interrupts these fixations on despair with an alternative logic drawn from the extravagant abundance of giving and receiving glory in praise and thanksgiving. Through doxologies of praise and thanksgiving, we are drawn into something larger than ourselves: the excessive round of joy that is the Trinity.

More than this, the joy emerging from the dynamics of glory is more than the affective assurance that things are not meant to be this way and will not be this way forever: joy energizes efforts to improve the present. Accordingly, in his commentary on Galatians, Luther describes joy in terms of duty: "When this is a joy of the Spirit, not of the flesh, the heart

---

22. Rivera, "Glory," 176. As Mary Clark Moschella writes in *Caring for Joy*, "We might think that joy is found in wealth or achievement, but instead it turns up in prisons and political protest movements" (229).

23. Mathewes, "Toward a Theology of Joy," 77.

rejoices inwardly through faith in Christ, because it knows for a certainty that He is our Savior and High Priest; and outwardly it demonstrates this joy in words and action."[24] For Luther, joy is both a feeling and an action. It is both affective and effective as the feeling of joy charges the body to spread joy in the theater of God's glory. Joy is something fundamental, therefore, to how we orient ourselves in the world. As Mary Clark Moschella says, joy "can strengthen our resolve to transform unjust social arrangements."[25] Part of that work is the disempowering of the dominant hold despair has over the imagination and the liberative possibilities that come from daring a different perspective on the world. A good part of that work is also recognizing that joy *is* "work," the hard labor of finding spaces for joy in the midst of massive temptations to be overcome by despair.

As a fruit of the Spirit, joy is a sign of glory at work in the world and present in our lives. Barth urges us to "consider carefully that real joy comes and is present like the Holy Spirit." Therefore, "we cannot create or construct or produce or force it."[26] There are certainly those occasions when we are provoked into joy by what is not of our "own doing" (Eph. 2:8)—supremely, the provocation of being created. To be fully alive involves the daily decision to lean into the dynamics of glory in responsive participation in the joy that is given to us, unearned. But there are other occasions when the most pressing need is for us to make time and space for joy. These are the spaces of emotional and spiritual habitation, and also geographical spaces—actual spaces carved out for joy. These abundantly joyous spaces, full of joyful noises to the Lord (Ps. 100:1), gather people together to respair against despair and energize bodies to lament into action by working against anything that blocks the joyous flow of glory in the world.

Embodying Glory

In the previous section, under an affective expansion of Irenaeus's dictum, we said there is no experience of glory that is not, at heart, an experience of joy. Joy covers the full semantic range of glory: it is the experience of abundance, overflow, intensity, and completeness. The glory of God is being joy-fully alive. One might think that to be fully alive—that is, to be

24. Luther, *Lectures on Galatians*, 93.
25. Moschella, *Caring for Joy*, xiii.
26. Barth, *CD* III/4, 379.

glorified and "filled with all the fullness of God" (Eph. 3:19)—would be the ultimate for anyone. What can exceed being full of God's joy? Where can you go after fullness? The doxological ethic of abundance and excess, which is central to our account of glorification, means that there is more even than completion, more than fullness, more than "more."

In this section we turn to the embodiment of glory to suggest that a sign of glory is the Spirit of glory resting on, and so glorifying, the body as the smile. As Stephen Pattison puts it, "The symbol of the human person fully alive is the smiling face."[27] So much of social life, human interaction, identity, and meaning is underpinned by the smile. The chemical reactions, the contraction of muscles, the turning of the lips, and the tightening of the cheeks that combine to give each smile its unrepeatable particularity; the physiology, anatomy, neurology, psychology, and sociology of the smile—all this is well documented. But what does a thing so ordinary as a smile have to do with a theme with such gravitas as glory?

Smiling

The face—divine and human—has attracted significant theological interest and is especially important when it comes to glory.[28] As Barth writes, "God's face is more than the radiance of light. And God's glory is the glory of His face, indeed His face itself, God in person, God who bears a name and calls us by name. God is glorious in the fact that He does this, that He reaches us in this way, that He Himself comes to us to be known by us."[29] Many of the key glory texts in the Bible involve faces. Moses's face was changed after encountering the presence of God's glory. Paul speaks of how the glory of God shines on the face of Jesus (2 Cor. 4:6). At the transfiguration, Matthew has the disciples fall facedown as the Son's face shines like the sun (17:6). And Christian living, also according to Paul, is a life of being faced with the face of Christ, in whose face we face the glory of God (2 Cor. 3:18). The face connects biblically with joy too. When the psalmist prays, "In your presence [*paneh*] there is

27. Pattison, *Saving Face*, 77.

28. See Ford, *Self and Salvation*, 167–90, for sustained reflection on face and facing, especially for an engagement with face, and face-to-face encounter, in the French philosopher Emmanuel Levinas's thought on human sociality; and Ford, *The Shape of Living*, 99–101, for a short reflection on the smile of Thérèse of Lisieux.

29. Barth, *CD* II/1, 647.

fullness of joy" (Ps. 16:11) and "You make him glad with the joy of your presence [*paneh*]" (21:6), the Hebrew word translated as "presence" can mean "face" as well. Here, as God faces us with the presence of glory, our bodies are charged with joy.

While "face" and "facing" have always been theologically generative, the smile is a more unusual focus of theological reflection. Every angle of the smile has been explored by every relevant discipline, but the smile has seemed to pass theologians by. Theological interest in the face tends to be in the phenomenon of the face rather than its physiological features. As John M. Hull puts it, "For [Emmanuel] Levinas, the face does not smile or frown, it is not a face with a specific gender, nor is it a singing face."[30]

That there is no explicit reference to Jesus smiling in the Gospels might go some way to account for the lack of much theological interest in the smile. We know Jesus wept, but there is no mention of the historical Jesus or his disciples smiling. The art historian Paul Binski goes further in arguing that "no one in the canon of 'authentic' early Christian religious literature smiles."[31] When excavating the emotional interiority of the life of Jesus, the Christian tradition has found more meaning in the Man of Sorrows, the Jesus who suffered and suffers alongside others, than the Man of Smiles.[32] References to the smiling Jesus in texts for prayer and liturgical resources are similarly limited. And the smiling Jesus has not been picked up by many poets or hymn writers or visual artists in the way, say, the "holy smile" of the Buddha is a firm fixture in Buddhist religious culture.

30. Hull, *The Tactile Heart*, 56.
31. Binski, "Angel Choir," 350.
32. An argument could be made that since smiling is so ordinary and such an unremarkable characteristic of being human, Jesus's smiles went unsaid. We know, of course, that Jesus enjoyed encounter with others, table fellowship, feasting, and the celebration and festivity of weddings—all things that would bring joy to hearts and smiles to faces. This position is supported by smile science informed by basic emotion and fixed facial expression theory. For a classic statement of this position, see Ekman, "Duchenne and Facial Expression." But there is also a chance that the Gospels don't describe Jesus as smiling because the smile did not carry the same social meaning then as it does today—at least in the context in which we are writing. The lack of a smiling Jesus in the Gospels is a reminder at least that smiling is culturally variable—then as now. This is the rough argument Mary Beard makes in response to the perceived lack of social significance of the smile in Roman literary culture; see *Laughter in Ancient Rome*, 73–81. Beard's position is also supported in smile science; see, for example, L. Barrett et al., "Emotional Expressions Reconsidered."

One exception is Godly Play's retelling of Genesis 1.[33] On the first day, after God had created light and darkness, Godly Play has an "enormous smile" on the face of God as God rejoices in the beauty of creation.[34] In the beginning was the smile. Indeed, in God's creating through speech, not conflict, it could even be said that God created through a smile as well as with a smile. When God peaceably called all things into existence, he spoke with a voiced smile. The voiced smile is an important part of the repertoire of smiling, especially in an age of masks.

The psychoanalyst Kenneth Wright would likely say that the association of the one who creates with the one who smiles "from above" taps into "that storehouse of early experience deep within the preverbal core of the self where the mother's face 'shines' (smiles) upon the baby in her arms and fills its whole perceptual world with light."[35] Some of the thematic connection between the smiling of the face and the shining of light is suggested when we speak today of a "beaming" or a "glowing" smile. There is even a minority textual tradition that translates the Hebrew word for shining as "smiling."[36] So when the Bible talks of God's face "shining," as it does with some regularity through the Old Testament and especially in the Psalms, this could be taken as a reference to the smile that was there in the beginning, as picked up by Godly Play. Pattison supports the possibility of such an interpretation when he asks, "What is the shining face of God but the smiling face of God?"[37] The New Living Translation follows this interpretive tradition, where we read in the Psalms:

Many people say, "Who will show us better times?" Let your face smile on us, LORD. (Ps. 4:6 NLT)

May God be merciful and bless us. May his face smile with favor on us. (Ps. 67:1 NLT)

33. Godly Play is a form of spiritual formation for children centered on story, wonder, imagination, and play.

34. Berryman, *Complete Guide to Godly Play*, 2:45. The idea might not be as outlandish as it sounds. According to the creation myth in a third-century BCE Egyptian papyrus, in the beginning was the laugh. The Egyptian Creator "confronts Chaos and laughs it off, delivering a world of joy and exuberance into the light." See B. Sanders, *Sudden Glory*, 1.

35. K. Wright, *Vision and Separation*, 19, quoted in Pattison, *Saving Face*, 86.

36. The NLT follows this tradition in its translation of the Psalms used below and, for example, of Num. 6:24–26 and Dan. 9:17.

37. Pattison, *Saving Face*, 86.

> Truth springs up from the earth, and righteousness smiles down from heaven. (Ps. 85:11 NLT)

Once "shining" gets interpreted as "smiling," the smiling face of God becomes associated with some of the most important words in glory's semantic field: *light, illumination, revelation, salvation, love, grace, blessing, restoration.* It also brings new meaning to hymns and songs featuring shining faces. "Shine, Jesus, Shine" would become "Smile, Jesus, smile / Fill this land with the Father's glory," as if to say the smiling face of Jesus, as the smile of God incarnate, is the radiating presence of the glory of God in the world. As with hymns and songs, such an interpretation brings new meaning to other shining faces in the Bible. When we read that Moses came down from Mount Sinai, what if we think of his shining face as a smiling face? It was not that he grew horns as a sign of the transformation that comes from God's glory resting on his body, but he grew, as Chagall knew, a smile. In one of Chagall's depictions of the burning bush scene, he has Moses's face not hiding but smiling—transfigured into a radiant, beautiful smile.[38] And what about when Jesus went up the mountain to pray and "the appearance of his face changed" (Luke 9:29)? This might be a sighting of the Man of Smiles.

As for the smile in Christian material culture, depictions of the smile were few and far between until around the mid-thirteenth century and the advent of the "Gothic Smile" movement.[39] All of a sudden and all around northern Europe, the Virgin Mary learned to smile, and with her the whole company of heaven (such as Lincoln Cathedral's Angel Choir and the angels on the west facade of Notre-Dame de Reims), the elect (such as the Last Judgment Portal at Bamberg Cathedral), and the prophets (such as the statue of Daniel on the Portico of Glory in the Santiago de Compostela Cathedral). Here, at the destination of one of the most important pilgrimage routes in the medieval world, the pilgrim would be greeted with the smile of a prophet of God. Dante, writing in southern Europe around the same time and influenced by the Gothic Smile movement that was taking hold in the north, goes further than smiling prophets in his unusual exploration of the smile shared "within" the divine life of God. According

---

38. Marc Chagall, *Moses and the Burning Bush* (1966).
39. See Binski, "Angel Choir."

to Peter Hawkins, the smile is "Dante's signature gesture," with references in the *Divine Comedy* increasing in frequency the closer the poet gets to the chief end of his own pilgrimaging to paradise.[40] The universe smiles, the lady smiles, Gregory smiles, Beatrice smiles, and *God smiles*. Dante not only speaks of smiles along the way to paradise, which accompany and encourage him, but once arrived he will behold the smile of God. In the closing canto (*Paradiso* 33.124–26), we read the poet praising God as the one who smiles upon himself, again with reference to shining light:

> Eternal light, you sojourn in yourself alone.
> Alone, you know yourself. Known to yourself,
> you, knowing, love and smile on your own being.[41]

The chief end of the Christian life is a smile, God's smile. For Dante, the "inner life of the Trinity, of God's own self, is nothing less than the sharing of a smile."[42]

As well as ending with the smile, the Christian life begins in smiles too. Possibly too much already has been made of the first smiles of a child and the role the smile plays in early development and socialization. Whether the smile is instinctive or imitative or more likely both, there is broad agreement among developmental psychologists that the emotional formation of a child begins with a smile.[43] Likewise, Balthasar, whose theological anthropology starts from the image of a mother and baby sharing a smile, writes, "In the mother's smile, it dawns on him that there is a world into which he is accepted and in which he is welcome, and it is in this primordial experience that he becomes aware of himself for the first time."[44] This suggests the intriguing idea that alongside the tradition of Jesus being taught to read by his mother as Mary was herself taught to read by her mother (as discussed in chap. 1), perhaps Mary also taught Jesus to smile. Jesus learned to smile as Mary smiled upon him, filling his whole perceptual world with light and joy, just as Mary's mother filled her life with joyous light through her smile.

---

40. Hawkins, "All Smiles," 53.
41. Dante Alighieri, *Divine Comedy*, 481.
42. Hawkins, "All Smiles," 52.
43. Messinger and Moffitt, "Smiling."
44. Balthasar, *Mary*, 102–3.

In one of his diary entries, John Hull reflects on his experience of sharing a smile with his young daughter. The entry of March 21, 1986, reads,

Yesterday morning I was kneeling on the floor helping Lizzie to get dressed. When she had finished, I stood her up in front of me and said, "Now! Let's have a look at you." I held her face lightly between my hands, and gave her a big smile. We remained like that for a moment and then she said, "Daddy, how can you smile between you and me when I smile and when you smile because you are blind?" I laughed, and said, "What do you mean darling? How can I what?" With great hesitation, and faltering over every word, she said, "How can you smile—no—how can I smile between you and me—no—between you and me a smile, when you're blind?" "You mean, how do I know when to smile at you?" "Yes," she said, "when you're blind." "It's true, darling," I said, "that blind people often don't know when to smile at people, and I often don't know when to smile at you, do I?" She agreed. "But today I knew you were smiling, darling, because you were standing there, and I was smiling at you, and I thought you were probably smiling at me. Were you?" Happily she replied, "Yes!"

So this little child, having just had her fourth birthday, is able to articulate the breakdown which blindness causes in the language of smiles. I noticed the fine distinction she made by the implication between smiling at someone and the smiling which takes place between people. I cannot describe my emotions as I reflected upon the fact that she had had so many experiences of smiling at me, but that the in-between smile was, for her and me, not only a great rarity, but a puzzle. I had endured a terrible loss and been granted a wonderful gain simultaneously.[45]

In the following section we explore further, in relation to the dynamics of glory, the "in-between" smile shared between others (Hull) and between the persons of the Godhead (Dante).

The Glory of the Smile

It is curious to think such an ordinary thing as a smile can be a sign of God's glory. Then again, in the sixteenth century Ignatius of Loyola taught that everything could be done for the glory of God, even the smallest and most dappled thing. In a similar way, in our time, Rivera

---

45. Hull, *Touching the Rock*, 153–54.

encourages attention to "the glory that flickers in the midst of everyday life."[46]

At the heart of this book is what we have been calling the dynamics of glory: the singular, radiating intensity of the glory shared "in between" God energetically attracts everything into its abundance. The smile can be interpreted according to these same dynamics. Perhaps most obviously, if joy is the most natural experience of glory, the smile is the prototypical expression of joy. The main insight from psychological research on the smile is the close association of the smile with the experience of joy. Of course, joy is expressed in a multiplicity of bodily ways (singing, leaping, dancing), and the smile can signal more than just joy; but for many cultures across the world and through history, the smile has long been associated with joy—it expresses, communicates, spreads, and even intensifies joy.[47]

We have said that glorification is characterized by a logic of abundance and intensification. Glory stretches all things into even more fullness. If nothing else, the smile describes the physical shape of this abundance. When a smile lights up a face, the face is stretched upward, quite literally. In Barth's terms, the glory that "upturns" prior conceptions of God also upturns the lips and the eyes as the muscles of the face rearrange themselves into the smile.[48] Moreover, the smile stretches the fullness of joy as the joy experienced in the heart overflows out of the body and into the world. How does the smile stretch joy? It intensifies it. The smile intensifies joy by making joy more joyous and the smiler more *fully* fully alive. And if the smile is a sign of creation delighting in God, as for Jürgen Moltmann "the laughter of the universe is God's delight," God delights in creation delighting.[49] There is a logic here of the smile perfecting the perfection of joy: the more we smile, the more God delights in our smiling with ever-intensifying waves of joyous glory flowing from the joyous round of love in the divine life, to which we respond with more joy, more delight, more smiles. More still, as there is no intrinsic need for the smile, the logics of the smile follow the logics of nonnecessity. The necessary is that which can-

46. Rivera, "Glory," 167.

47. The mid-nineteenth-century French experimental physiologist G.-B. Duchenne de Boulogne famously associated the facial expression of the smile with the basic emotion of joy. See Duchenne de Boulogne, *The Mechanism of Human Facial Expression*.

48. Barth, *Credo*, 12–13.

49. Moltmann, *The Coming of God*, 339.

not be otherwise. But there are other ways of communicating the feelings embodied in the smile—strangers could kiss in the street as the Romans did;[50] loved ones could embrace each other; other bodily gestures could give adequate expression to the joy that teems in the heart. The smile exists then, as glory exists, as superfluous in the best possible sense—for its own sake—and is consistent with what Eberhard Jüngel would call the "more than necessary," the extravagance and excess of abundance.[51]

The smile is radiantly attractive, flickering with evanescent beauty. When we speak of a beaming smile, we mean the way a smile not only gives external expression to internal feelings but also communicates—that is, *radiates*—something to the world. That something is the epiphany of joy. Moreover, the aesthetic of the smile, precisely in its radiation of joy, is attractive. The particularizing beauty of the smile is so entrancing that it evokes in others, often irresistibly and spontaneously, a response in kind: the smile returns a smile. When you smile at someone, they usually smile back. The smile begets a smile as glory begets glory. And to smile at someone and to see them smiling back is to "resonate" with them, to be affected by them and drawn deeper into their lives, however fleetingly.[52] To smile back is more than a response in kind. The smile returned is more than an echo, more than a repetition, more than mere mimicry. As the one smiled upon returns the gift of the smile with a smile, these smiles are mutually intensifying in such a way that is transformative. The completeness of my smile is further completed by the smile of another and by the sorts of relationality it inspires. When I smile, and you smile back, your smile does not take anything away from my smile. It is not that the more you smile, the less "smile" there is to go around. The smile's logic of abundance does not work with this model of scarcity but understands smiles to increase in equally intensifying proportions. The more a smile radiates, the more it attracts, and the more a smile is entranced by another smile, the more it becomes more fully itself. The exchange of smiles—the dynamic of giving

---

50. Beard, *Laughter in Ancient Rome*, 75.

51. See again Jüngel, *God as the Mystery of the World*, 24–35.

52. On the social significance of resonance, see again the work of the German sociologist Hartmut Rosa. The spontaneous smile would be a good case not only of what he calls the "uncontrollability of the world" but also of the resonance that is not just an echo of ourselves but genuine dialogue with the other. As well as Rosa's *Resonance* mentioned earlier, see *The Uncontrollability of the World*.

and receiving—leaves both smilers in a state of being different, having had their desires shaped through these dynamics of attraction.[53]

As intensely reflective of the self and extensively other-oriented, the smile follows the double dynamic of glory's journeying deeper into the self and deeper into relationship with others. It generates new relationships (such as the smile shared between strangers as they pass each other on the street), intensifies existing ones (such as the smile shared year after year with the same person), and heals damaged relationships. These relational exchanges are signs of glorification, flickers of glory in everyday life. Indeed, during the time of physical distancing, the sociality of the smile was for many the most intensive form of embrace possible—in both digital and nondigital life. In a world of despair, the smile images joy's anti-violent logic. It shows to a world of despair something that is good, spreading the joy that flows from the glory of God and respairing against all that blocks joy.

We have said that you cannot talk about glory without talking about the Spirit, the Spirit of glory; so too the glory of the smile. There are three pneumatological aspects of the glory of the smile to be discussed below: the ethics of encouragement, hospitality, and participation.

The Ethic of Encouragement

In his vivid and glory-centered writings on the Spirit, Pavel Florensky says that "the Holy Spirit has always been the Comforter, the Paraclete, the Bringer of Joy."[54] The smile, as a sign of the Spirit at work in the world,

---

53. Balthasar sees sacramental imagery in the smile:

After a mother has smiled at her child for many days and weeks, she finally receives her child's response. She has awakened love in the heart of her child. . . . God interprets himself to man as love in the same way: he radiates love, which kindles the light of love in the heart of man, and it is precisely this light that allows man to perceive this, the absolute Love: "For it is God who said, 'Let light shine out of the darkness,' who has shone in our heart to give the light of the knowledge of the glory of God in the face of Christ" (2 Cor. 4:6). In this face, the primal foundation of being smiles at us as a mother and as a father. Insofar as we are his creatures, the sea of love lies dormant within us as the image of God (*imago*). But just as no child can be awakened to love without being loved, so too no human heart can come to an understanding of God without the free gift of his grace—in the image of his Son. (Balthasar, *Love Alone Is Credible*, 76)

54. Florensky, *The Pillar and Ground of the Truth*, 102.

has an extraordinary capacity to comfort and bring joy to the lives of those smiled upon. Indeed, a rich ethic of encouragement radiates from the face of Beatrice, so often the figure of the Spirit in Dante's poetry and the one who smiles the most. More than any other, it is the smile of Beatrice in which Dante finds most encouragement and comfort. "Beatrice's smile *is* the way that Dante journeys toward the beatific vision of God."[55] If glorification is the end, the beginning of the end is the doxological ethic of comforting, blessing, and encouraging others on their journeying into the deepening depths of divine glory. Following the minority textual tradition mentioned earlier, the comforting words of the blessing God instructs Moses to teach Aaron, which forms the Benediction given at the end of Christian worship, expresses the divine origins of this ethic of comforting:

> May the LORD bless you
>> and protect you.
> May the LORD smile on you
>> and be gracious to you.
> May the LORD show you his favor
>> and give you his peace. (Num. 6:24–26 NLT)

THE ETHIC OF HOSPITALITY

The smile, as the face is for Levinas, is a sign of the irreducible singularity of the self.[56] In its evasion of easy representation, its unrepeatable particularity, its total uniqueness, the smile comes to indicate the massive assurance that there is always more to us than the qualities and attributes ascribed to us. There is always more to life than the roles we play in church and at work and the positions we hold in society and in the economy. The smile says that life depends above all on the call of God, who calls us into lives full of joy. Also for Levinas, as the part of the body most regularly exposed to the world, as extensively other-oriented, the smile faces the world. And the smiling face is the face at its most hospitable, enlightened by the holy hospitality of the Spirit. There is an eloquence of the smile that while so supremely intimate is also dynamically oriented toward the other. The smile of joy signifies the generosity of welcome, unbounded

---

55. Hawkins, "All Smiles," 47.
56. See Morgan, *Cambridge Introduction to Emmanuel Levinas*.

inclusion, unconditional hospitality, and the active seeking of possibilities for loving resonance with others central to doxological living.

THE ETHIC OF PARTICIPATION

The exchange of the smile follows a triadic logic between the smiler, the smile, and the one smiled upon. Analogous to the Spirit's work as the bond of love between the Father and the Son is the smile's work of uniting—"oneing," to use again Julian's glorious term—the smiler and the one smiled upon in a loving relationship of togetherness and ever-deepening levels of intensification. Augustine might recognize the exchange of the smile, and the sort of relationality it inspires, as an analogy of the Trinity: that which loves, that which is loved, and love itself are analogous to that which smiles, that which is smiled upon, and the smile itself. If the smile is governed by a lived dynamic of abundance, it comes to reflect, like memory, the inner logic of the Trinity and in so doing images, however flickeringly, something of the glory of God to the world.

There is always a danger, however, that the concept of the Spirit as the "bond" of union puts the stress on what is being bonded and not on the bond itself. More helpful to emphasize the smile in and of itself is the full-bodied pneumatology Eugene Rogers develops in *After the Spirit*. Rogers argues that "to think about the Spirit it will not do to think 'spiritually': to think about the Spirit you have to think materially"—and this means thinking about the Spirit in relation to bodies.[57] As the Spirit rested on (and so glorified) the body of Christ, the Spirit rests on our bodies as glory and glorifies our flesh. "Theologically speaking, the body becomes a channel through which God can reveal Godself, the Spirit can perform her appropriated office of divine manifestation."[58] As the Spirit rests on bodies, we might add that the Spirit comes to rest on the face as the gift of the smile. For Rogers, "the Spirit characteristically befriends the body," here and now, and in so doing joins the human person to the trinitarian life just as in joy we are joined "with" the glorious joy of God.[59] From Rogers we can speak of the work of the Spirit as crucial for expressing not only how trinitarian relations might be imaged to the world through the dynamics

57. Rogers, *After the Spirit*, 56.
58. Rogers, *After the Spirit*, 184.
59. Rogers, *After the Spirit*, 60.

of the smile but also how the smile is a sign of being incorporated into the trinitarian nature of God. More specifically, the dynamics of glory suggest that the Spirit incorporates us into the smile of the glorified Christ, the "prototype of all doxology."[60]

The doxological postlude marking the end of this book is Graham Sutherland's *Christ in Glory in the Tetramorph*, which dominates the north end of Coventry Cathedral behind the high altar. When you first enter the new cathedral, having moved through ruins of the old, you are faced with the face of Christ, in whom the glory of God is encountered. The liturgical choreography of the cathedral means that when those gathered together for Holy Communion draw near with faith and move to face the glorified face of Christ, they are attracted deeper into the dynamics of Christ's face. As you get closer and notice more of its expressiveness, you see flickering on the face of Christ a smile. It is not a complete smile, but there is the unmistakable beginning of a smile that nevertheless dazzles. For Balthasar, the smile of Jesus reveals to the world the smile of God that was there before the foundation of the world. "The very ground of being," he says, "smiles upon us in the face of Christ, as a father or mother might smile at us."[61] The smiling face of Jesus is even more radiant when set against the facelessness of the figure clamped at his feet. It is not that the faceless figure at the feet of Christ has been defaced, as it were. The figure at the feet of Christ is not so much faceless as formless, ready to be formed from one degree of glory to another (1 Cor. 3:18). Like the faceless figure standing at the feet of the glorified Christ ready to be formed for glory, when we smile, we "put on" (Gal. 3:26–27) the smile of the glorified Christ, not simply imitating but assimilating Christ's smile, and so come to rest in God as the Spirit of glory rests on our bodies as the smile. We smile as we pray, that is, "by His mouth," Calvin would say.[62] When heaven and earth are full of God's glory, all things will be all smiles, and until that end the smile comes to manifest something of that destiny: to be effective signs of God's grace and justice, enacting glory in the world. "Might not . . . the end for which humankind was made, be the infinite mirroring of God's smile?"[63]

60. Barth, *CD* IV/3, 48.
61. Balthasar, *Love Alone Is Credible*, 62.
62. Calvin, *Catechism of the Church of Geneva* (1545), 122.
63. Hawkins, "All Smiles," 53.

Enacting Glory

"And on the seventh day God finished the work that he had done, and he rested on the seventh day from all the work that he had done. So God blessed the seventh day and hallowed it, because on it God rested from all the work that he had done in creation" (Gen. 2:2–3). In the Bible the Sabbath is there at the culmination of creation, as the first full day lived by human beings. The humans have already been blessed and given work and responsibilities, and, at the end of the sixth day, "God saw everything that he had made, and indeed, it was very good" (Gen. 1:31).

It is hard to imagine what could be added to what God finds very good, but there is more. The complete creation is to be completed. There is an overflow of the work of God in creation that is described as God blessing and hallowing the seventh day because he was resting. Blessing and hallowing are therefore not to be considered work, and rest can embrace activities that come under the heading of blessing and hallowing. Rest is clearly freedom from work; it is also freedom for things relating to blessing and hallowing. Freedom for what?

The biblical kinship between blessing, hallowing, and glorifying has become clear in previous chapters, and it resonates further (most intensively and exuberantly in the Psalms) through activities such as praising, thanking, singing and dancing, proclaiming, testifying, confessing, celebrating, lifting up and exalting, extolling, magnifying, delighting, adoring, loving, trusting, invoking and naming, crying out, hoping, wondering, being amazed and astonished, laughing, experiencing peace, enjoying abundance, and, as earlier in this chapter, rejoicing, as well as through the shining and smiling of faces. If glorifying and such kindred activities are to characterize the lives of communities and their members, then they would be wise to take seriously and joyfully the importance of the Sabbath. We all need special times of and spaces for overflow, celebration, and freedom for what is most important besides the necessities of work.

The Bible places an extraordinary emphasis on the Sabbath. It is not only the culmination of creation, imprinted in the shape of time itself and directly related to the blessing, hallowing, and resting of God (in a way that "natural" markers of time such as light and darkness, sun and moon are not); it is also at the heart of the Sinai covenant, as expressed in the Ten Commandments.[64]

There is an instructive difference between the two versions of the Ten Commandments. In Exodus 20 it is "Remember the sabbath day, and keep it holy. Six days you shall labor and do all your work. But the seventh day is a sabbath to the LORD your God; you shall not do any work—you, your son or your daughter, your male or female slave, your livestock, or the alien resident in your towns. For in six days the LORD made heaven and earth, the sea, and all that is in them, but rested the seventh day; therefore the LORD blessed the sabbath day and consecrated it" (vv. 8–11). The version in Deuteronomy 5 begins like Exodus but then, where Exodus grounds the Sabbath in creation, Deuteronomy appeals to the exodus from Egypt: "Remember that you were a slave in the land of Egypt, and the LORD your God brought you out from there with a mighty hand and an outstretched arm; therefore the LORD your God commanded you to keep the sabbath day" (v. 15).

So there is an appeal not only to creation but also to the climactic event in the formation of Israel as a people who are in a covenantal relationship with God: their liberation from slavery in Egypt. Keeping the Sabbath builds into life the centrality of God as both the creator who is to be blessed and who blesses and the liberator who is on the side of those in history who are politically, economically, or otherwise enslaved or oppressed. God's concern is also with nonhuman animals, and the land too is included in an ecological vision that includes giving it rest from being overworked: "The land shall observe a sabbath for the LORD" (Lev. 25:2).

Beyond creation and the Ten Commandments, there is also a prophetic passion for the Sabbath. Isaiah 56 and 58 are especially important.[65] There, not only is the Sabbath essential to the whole covenantal relationship of Israel with God, especially to living with justice (56:1;

64. In Genesis, just as "in the beginning" (1:1) light is created first by God before the "natural" givers of light and markers of time (sun, moon, and stars), so when "God finished the work that he had done" (2:2), there is a sign, the Sabbath, that is not directly related to such natural markers (as are seasons and each day) but solely the result of the desire, generosity, and word of God. Through history, keeping the Sabbath has been both a sign of rejection of the worship of natural entities represented by sun, moon, or stars (or any other "idol") and a challenge to one culture and civilization after another regarding their shaping of time and the priorities their particular shape carries with it.

65. See also Jer. 17; Ezek. 20, 22, 46.

58:1–6), generosity (58:7, 9, 10, 13), and compassion (58:7, 10), but its covenantal wisdom, blessing, glory (58:8), and joy (58:13–14) can be had by unlikely, marginalized people within Israel, such as eunuchs, and by foreigners. There is here a Sabbath-centered joining of creation-wide universality with the particularity of Israel, as in the two versions of the Ten Commandments:

> And the foreigners who join themselves to the LORD,
>   to minister to him, to love the name of the LORD,
>   and to be his servants,
> all who keep the sabbath, and do not profane it,
>   and hold fast my covenant—
> these I will bring to my holy mountain,
>   and make them joyful in my house of prayer;
> their burnt offerings and their sacrifices
>   will be accepted on my altar;
> for my house shall be called a house of prayer
>   for all peoples.
> Thus says the Lord GOD,
>   who gathers the outcasts of Israel,
> I will gather others to them
>   besides those already gathered. (Isa. 56:6–8)

In the New Testament there is considerable emphasis on universality, as when Jesus expels money changers and merchants from the temple, quoting Isaiah 56 (Mark 11:15–19).[66] Jesus assumes observance of the Sabbath, and throughout the New Testament there is no questioning its importance. The questions arise about how it is to be observed. In the context of the debates among fellow Jews in his day, Jesus sides with those who allow acts of compassion, such as his healings on the Sabbath.

But his most radical statement is given in response to criticism of his hungry disciples for plucking and eating grain as they walked through grainfields on the Sabbath. "The sabbath was made for humankind, and not humankind for the sabbath; so the Son of Man is lord even of the sabbath" (Mark 2:27–28; cf. Matt. 12:1–8; Luke 5:33–39). This focus on his authority, and on who he is, is in line with the radicality of what

---

66. Only Mark includes the reference to all the nations or peoples. Cf. Matt. 21:12–17; Luke 19:45–46; John 2:13–22.

he says and does elsewhere in relation to Scripture, forgiveness, exorcism, raising the dead, healing, the natural world, and, above all, the kingdom of God and God as his Father.[67] Often, the response to him is gratitude and amazement that overflows into praising and glorifying God.

In Mark's Gospel, probably the earliest, this note is emphatically struck from the beginning. "They were astounded at his teaching.... They were all amazed, and they kept on asking one another, 'What is this?' ... They were all amazed and glorified God" (Mark 1:22, 27; 2:12). Doxology is a response not only to what Jesus says and does but also to who he is. That "what" question involves a "who" question. "'Who can forgive sins but God alone?' ... And they were filled with great awe and said to one another, 'Who then is this, that even the wind and the sea obey him?'" (Mark 2:7; 4:41).

In the Gospel of John, probably the latest, such response is summed up in a key verse of the Prologue, 1:14: "We have seen his glory." Then, as discussed in chapter 2 of this book, the theme of glory is sustained throughout the rest of this Gospel. All the "signs" Jesus does in his public ministry come under this heading, from the first one, which "revealed his glory" at a wedding in Cana (2:11), to the last one, the raising of Lazarus from death: "This illness does not lead to death; rather it is for God's glory, so that the Son of God may be glorified through it" (11:4; cf. 11:40).

The rest of the Gospels of Mark and John, together with the Gospels of Matthew and Luke and the rest of the New Testament, overwhelmingly testifies to the glory of God in Jesus Christ. Jesus is God's glory in person. He acts doxologically; he speaks doxologically; he prays, lives, and dies doxologically; and his resurrection is the decisive revelation of his glory. His disciples too need to learn doxological action, doxological speech, doxological prayer, doxological living, and, if necessary, doxological dying—all as followers of the crucified, resurrected, glorified Jesus.[68] The question now is, What practice of the Sabbath might that following invite and inspire?

---

67. The Gospel of John does not have the grainfield event or the accompanying saying but, as so often, offers something that can open up their "deep plain sense." In this case, see John 5, 7, and 9 on Sabbath disputes that lead into profound statements on the authority of Jesus and who he is in relation to his Father. See Ford, *Gospel of John*, 165–67.

68. For example, what the resurrected Jesus says to Peter "to indicate the kind of death by which he would glorify God" is followed immediately by "Follow me" (John 21:19).

Most but not all Christians around the world today observe Sunday as their Sabbath, and it is worth reflecting on why this is so. The main reason seems to be that the early church came to celebrate the Lord's Supper (or Eucharist, or Mass) on Sunday as the day of the resurrection of Jesus. This makes deep sense, but it also makes deep sense that other Christians (including some Jewish Christians, Seventh Day Baptists, and Seventh-day Adventists) observe the Sabbath on Saturday (or when most Jews observe it, from Friday evening till Saturday evening).

Perhaps the most illuminating approach to the question posed above is through the idea of ongoing completion and overflow, as already seen in this chapter in relation to the Sabbath completing an already complete creation and the smile completing an already fully full experience of joy. The New Testament strongly emphasizes the death of Jesus on Good Friday as a completion, something that has happened on the cross "once for all."[69] How, then, do we regard the following two days, Holy Saturday and Easter Sunday? Like the Sabbath of Genesis 2:2–3, they can be seen together as the completion of that "once for all" death, and even as a time of "new creation" (2 Cor. 5:17). Both days are essential to this completing of the completion—the blessing, hallowing, and glorifying that flow from the crucified Jesus.[70] Both days became, with the day of the crucifixion of Jesus, the "hour" (see Mark 14:41; John 12:23) that defines the shape of Christian time: the climax of the Christian year is at the end of Holy Week in Good Friday, Holy Saturday, and Easter Sunday. All three days are also essential to baptism. "Do you not know that all of us who have been baptized into Christ Jesus were baptized into his death? Therefore we have been buried with him by baptism into death, so that, just as Christ was raised from the dead by the glory of the Father, so we too might walk in newness of life" (Rom. 6:3–4).

So the main time defining the Christian community and the main time defining the core identity of each Christian includes the Sabbath, whether it is celebrated on Saturday or Sunday. The deep wisdom and

69. The Gospel of John (especially 19:30: "It is finished") and the Letter to the Hebrews (9:12, 26; 10:10, 12) are especially insistent on this.

70. This is vividly expressed in the Gospel of John by Jesus, who, as soon as he says, "It is finished," hands over "the spirit/Spirit" (on this, see Ford, *Gospel of John*, 385–88) and then, on Easter Sunday, breathes the Holy Spirit into his disciples (20:22). It is also symbolized by the piercing of the side of the dead Jesus, from which "blood and water came out" (19:34).

massive imperative of Sabbath observance are, if anything, intensified by the death and resurrection of Jesus. The Sabbath enacts the temporal shape of abundance, just as joy is an experience of its affective shape and smiling embodies its physical shape.

The Sabbath is the culmination of creation in Genesis 2:2–3, and the Ten Commandments ground it there; and the most comprehensive analogy to Jesus Christ being "raised from the dead by the glory of the Father" is the action of God in creation, which in turn overflows into the "newness of life" and baptized identity of Christians: "If anyone is in Christ, there is a new creation" (2 Cor. 5:17). The Ten Commandments also ground the Sabbath in the exodus from Egypt; and Jesus in his conversation with Moses and Elijah on the Mount of Transfiguration speaks of his "departure [*exodos*], which he was about to accomplish at Jerusalem" (Luke 9:31), an exodus that coincided with the feast of the Passover, remembering and reenacting the exodus from Egypt.

So what is being celebrated by followers of Jesus is a new creation and a new exodus. The character of their core celebration was set by Jesus himself at the Last Supper: "Do this in remembrance of me" (1 Cor. 11:24; cf. Matt. 26:26–28; Mark 14:22–24; Luke 22:17–20; John 6:41–58). In addition, there is an irresistible implication: the Sabbath is to be celebrated. The one through whom "all things came into being" (John 1:3) does not undo the culmination of creation. The one who is lord of the Sabbath does not cancel it. Rather, the Sabbath is renewed and comes to be called "the Lord's day."

Which day? It is easy to understand the case for continuing with Saturday, supported by Torah, the prophets, the practice of Jesus, and the example of his followers on the final pre-resurrection Saturday. "On the sabbath they rested according to the commandment" (Luke 23:56). Yet it is also easy to understand how the resurrection experience of the following day made Sunday the day of celebration par excellence. We see both days as essential to Christian time and identity. There is even, we suggest, something appropriate in some Christians, with good reason, deciding for each. It helps shift the focus from which day is called the Sabbath to what the Sabbath is meant to be: a special time each week in which there is freedom from work and freedom for other things that resonate with blessing, holiness, and glory and are in line with who Jesus, the lord of the Sabbath, is.

Even beyond a special day each week, and without at all taking away from the importance of a Sabbath that is a full day, both Jews (for whom it is twenty-five hours) and Christians have found that observing such a day can affect all other days and all time. The wisdom of resting, blessing, hallowing, and glorifying has led to a range of practices and spiritualities that combine anticipating the Sabbath, celebrating the Sabbath, appreciating the overflow of the Sabbath, and recognizing or creating signs of the Sabbath.[71]

There can be "little Sabbaths" in the day or the night. There are doxological moments in which the glory of God and the abundance of life God gives are recognized and celebrated in some way. In terms of this chapter, one might think of moments of joy when the heart leaps at a sight, sound, scent, taste, touch, memory, anticipation, or encounter; or when one pauses to savor something or someone with delight; or in the exchanging of smiles. There can also be more intentional times through the day amounting to practices and habits that interrupt work or other everyday occupations with breakout time, silence, rest, recollection, prayer, thanks, or praise. Mature doxological living in the presence of God has always valued and cultivated such practices and habits. These are about the pattern of daily and weekly life, taking into account night and day; rhythms of work, leisure, and sleep; periods of retreat or holiday; times of prayer; types of household and community; and the preciousness of the Sabbath day itself. The wisdom of the Sabbath also extends beyond the day and the week to the seasons and their festivals;[72] to lifetimes (which can be punctuated by "sabbatical" periods of various sorts); to communities across generations;

---

71. For a profound and prophetic theology of the Sabbath, set within a full Jewish theology from which Christians have much else to learn too, see Goshen-Gottstein, *In God's Presence*.

72. The annual cycle of biblical festivals, as laid down in Lev. 23, is headed by the Sabbath (v. 3), and the festivals that follow sometimes begin and end in Sabbaths and are pervaded by Sabbath-like observance: "You shall not work at your occupations" (vv. 7, 8, 21, 25, 35, 36; cf. v. 39); and, even more insistently, the Day of Atonement is to be strictly observed: "You shall do no work during that entire day. . . . Anyone who does any work during that entire day, such a one I will destroy from the midst of the people. . . . It shall be to you a sabbath of complete rest, and you shall deny yourselves; on the ninth day of the month at evening, from evening to evening you shall keep your sabbath" (vv. 28–32). Besides this Sabbath-saturated annual cycle, there is also the land's "sabbath for the LORD" every seventh year (Lev. 25:1–7); and "count[ing] off seven weeks of years, seven times seven years," there is, after every forty-nine years, the Year of Jubilee (25:8–55). In this the land lies fallow, property that has had to be sold is returned to the family that sold it, burdens of debt are relieved,

and to the ultimate vision of eternally living, loving, and rejoicing in the presence of God, each other, and God's glorious creation, as desired by Jesus in his climactic prayer: "Father, I desire that those also, whom you have given me, may be with me where I am, to see my glory, which you have given me because you loved me before the foundation of the world" (John 17:24). What has flowed from this love, and is now sustained by this love, is the whole of created reality. The glory of God is this creation fully alive through blessing and being blessed in wisdom, love, and joy, and the Sabbath is a rich image of ongoing, ever-overflowing fulfillment. In its variety of forms it can be a sign of the abundant life that Jesus, the lord of the Sabbath, came to bring (John 10:10), and its personal, social, economic, political, and ecological implications are endless.

This is not the place to develop an applied wisdom of the Sabbath, with its promise of immense practical blessings. It is sufficient to say that we are foolish if we ignore this wisdom, and that to attend to it, letting it help shape our communities and lives, is to receive a gift from God that is continually generative and fruitful. But this is certainly the place, at the culmination of our exploration of glorification, to seek the deepest root of the Sabbath in God's glory. A vital clue is in the phrase just quoted from John 17:24 about the glory shared with Jesus by his Father in love, "before the foundation of the world." That echoes the glory-saturated opening of the prayer, which leads into Jesus praying, "I glorified you on earth by finishing the work that you gave me to do. So now, Father, glorify me in your own presence with the glory that I had in your presence before the world existed" (17:4–5). For a biblical theological imagination, the connection with the Sabbath is clear. The finishing of the work of Jesus is accompanied by a glorifying that resonates with the blessing and hallowing that accompany God's finishing of creation in Genesis.[73] Yet not

---

people who have had to be sold as slaves are freed, and there are other provisions for a more just and compassionate society.

73. It is even clearer if one reads the Greek of John's Bible, the Septuagint. The "work" (Greek *ergon*) that Jesus finishes echoes the use of the same Greek word twice in Gen. 2:2–3 about God finishing his works in creation, and the verb "to do" (Greek *poiein*), used for Jesus finishing his work, is what the Septuagint uses for "create" or "make" (Gen. 1:1, 7, 16, 21, 25, 27, 31; 2:2 [twice], 3). There are other echoes of these Genesis verses too, above all in the emphasis on life (Greek *zōē*), which connects with the Johannine phrase "eternal life" (Greek *zōē aiōnion* and *aiōnios zōē* in 17:2, 3). Christian theology, liturgy, spirituality, hymns, literature, and art have often interrelated "eternal life," "eternal rest," and the Sabbath.

only that: here we are invited to think of the life of God "before the world existed," a life conceived as glorification. This is the ultimate origin of the whole of creation. But it is especially fitting to think of it in terms of the completion of creation in the Sabbath. In Genesis that is God's own special day, when God rests, blesses, and sanctifies.

And, as we have seen in chapter 2, John 17 not only testifies to the unimaginably deep, intense, creative, and abundant "eternal life" of divine glory; Jesus also says, "The glory that you have given me I have given them" (v. 22). This is the ultimate gift. We are invited and attracted into God's rest, blessing, holiness,[74] and glory. The wisdom of the Sabbath is rooted there, even deeper than the culmination of creation, in who God is in God's own glorious being, life, and love.

Sabbath time is when we are, above all, free to live doxologically, for the glory of God. It is about living "for God's sake," in utter devotion, desiring to love, glorify, and enjoy God with all our heart, mind, soul, and strength. Sabbath time overflows in all directions and affects the whole of life, and at its heart is enjoying God. It can be inhabited more and more fully through practices and habits, but only if these are rooted in who God is. The Psalms testify to this, as does Jewish worship down the centuries and today,[75] and also Christian worship—for example, in the *Gloria in Excelsis*:

> Glory to God in the highest,
> and peace to his people on earth.
> Lord God, heavenly King,
> almighty God and Father,
> we worship you, we give you thanks,
> we praise you for your glory.

74. Note the emphasis in John 17 on the sharing of holiness as well as glory and love: "Sanctify them in the truth; your word is truth. As you [the Father] have sent me into the world, so I have sent them into the world. And for their sakes I sanctify myself, so that they also may be sanctified in truth" (vv. 17–19).

75. The Jewish Sabbath liturgy exemplifies this. We are grateful to Alon Goshen-Gottstein for a personal communication, drawing on his magnum opus *In God's Presence*, that traces how glory explicitly and implicitly pervades the Sabbath liturgy. This is shown, for example, through Psalms, the orientation to God's kingdom and to the universal recognition of God's glory, recitation from Mishnah Shabbat, the acknowledgment of God's presence, and participation in God's glory. He concludes, "Glory is one of the gifts that God gives us and is the essence of Shabbat. Glory, then, would be one major feature of the Shabbat, along with holiness and rest, that are fundamental to the Shabbat's reality."

Lord Jesus Christ, only Son of the Father,
Lord God, Lamb of God,
you take away the sin of the world:
have mercy on us;
you are seated at the right hand of the Father:
receive our prayer.
For you alone are the Holy One,
you alone are the Lord,
you alone are the Most High, Jesus Christ,
with the Holy Spirit,
in the glory of God the Father.
Amen.

Earlier we posed the question "Freedom for what?" But the ultimate question is "Freedom for whom?" For God.

DOXOLOGICAL POSTLUDE

Christ in Glory in the Tetramorph
(Graham Sutherland, 1962)

Bibliography

Akala, Adesola Joan, ed. *Exploring the Glory of God: New Horizons for a Theology of Glory*. Lanham, MD: Rowman & Littlefield, 2021.

Alves, Rubem. *I Believe in the Resurrection of the Body*. Eugene, OR: Wipf & Stock, 1986.

Athanasius. *Four Discourses against the Arians*. In *Athanasius: Select Writings and Letters. Nicene and Post-Nicene Fathers*, Series 2, 4:303–447. Edinburgh: T&T Clark, 1892.

Balthasar, Hans Urs von. *The Glory of the Lord*. 7 vols. San Francisco: Ignatius, 1982–91.

———. *Love Alone Is Credible*. San Francisco: Ignatius, 2016.

———. *Mary: The Church at the Source*. San Francisco: Ignatius, 2005.

Barrett, Al. *Interrupting the Church's Flow: A Radically Receptive Political Theology in the Urban Margins*. London: SCM, 2020.

Barrett, Al, and Ruth Harley. *Being Interrupted: Reimagining the Church's Mission from the Outside, In*. London: SCM, 2020.

Barrett, Lisa Feldman, et al. "Emotional Expressions Reconsidered: Challenges to Inferring Emotion from Human Facial Movements." *Psychological Science in the Public Interest* 20, no. 1 (2019): 1–68.

Barth, Karl. *Church Dogmatics*. 4 vols. in 13 parts. Edited by G. W. Bromiley and T. F. Torrance. Edinburgh: T&T Clark, 1956–75.

———. *Credo*. London: Hodder & Stoughton, 1964.

———. *The Epistle to the Ephesians*. Grand Rapids: Baker Academic, 2017.

Bauckham, Richard. *Gospel of Glory: Major Themes in Johannine Theology*. Grand Rapids: Baker Academic, 2015.

———. "Joining Creation's Praise of God." *Journal for the Study of Religion, Nature and Culture* 7, no. 1 (2002): 45–59.

Beard, Mary. *Laughter in Ancient Rome: On Joking, Tickling, and Cracking Up*. Los Angeles: University of California Press, 2015.

Begbie, Jeremy. *Abundantly More: The Theological Promise of the Arts in a Reductionist World*. Grand Rapids: Baker Academic, 2023.

———. "Through Music: Sound Mix." In *Beholding the Glory: Incarnation through the Arts*, edited by Jeremy Begbie, 138–54. London: Darton, Longman & Todd, 2000.

Berger, Peter L. *Redeeming Laughter: The Comic Dimension of Human Experience*. Berlin: de Gruyter, 2014.

Berryman, Jerome W. *The Complete Guide to Godly Play*. Vol. 2. New York: Church Publishing, 2010.

Binski, Paul. "The Angel Choir at Lincoln and the Poetics of the Gothic Smile." *Art History* 20, no. 3 (1997): 350–74.

Bonhoeffer, Dietrich. *"Life Together" and "Prayerbook of the Bible."* Translated by Daniel W. Bloesch and James H. Burtness. Dietrich Bonhoeffer Works 5. Minneapolis: Fortress, 2004.

The Book of Common Prayer. New York: Oxford University Press, 1979.

Bourdieu, Pierre. *The Logic of Practice*. Stanford: Stanford University Press, 1990.

Brugarolas, Miguel. "The Holy Spirit as the 'Glory' of Christ: Gregory of Nyssa on John 17:22." In *The Ecumenical Legacy of the Cappadocians*, edited by Nicu Dumitraşcu, 247–63. New York: Palgrave Macmillan, 2016.

Brunner, Emil. *The Christian Doctrine of God*. Vol. 1 of *Dogmatics*. Philadelphia: Westminster, 1950.

Buckley, James. "The Rules for Scriptural Reasoning." *Journal of Scriptural Reasoning* 2, no. 1 (2002), https://jsr.shanti.virginia.edu/back-issues/volume-2-no-1-may -2002-the-rules-of-scriptural-reasoning/the-rules-of-scriptural-reasoning-5/.

Calvin, John. *Catechism of the Church of Geneva* (1545). In *Calvin: Theological Treatises*, edited by J. K. S. Reid, 88–139. Philadelphia: Westminster, 1960.

———. *The Epistles of Paul the Apostle to the Galatians, Ephesians, Philippians and Colossians*. Calvin's New Testament Commentaries 11. Grand Rapids: Eerdmans, 1996.

———. *The Gospel according to St. John 11–21*. Calvin's New Testament Commentaries 5. Grand Rapids: Eerdmans, 1996.

———. *Institutes of the Christian Religion*. Translated by Ford Lewis Battles. Philadelphia: Westminster John Knox, 1960.

Carvalhaes, Cláudio. *Liturgies from Below: Praying with People at the End of the World*. Nashville: Abingdon, 2020.

———. *What's Worship Got to Do with It? Interpreting Life Liturgically*. Eugene, OR: Cascade Books, 2018.

Coakley, Sarah. *God, Sexuality, and the Self: An Essay "On the Trinity."* Cambridge: Cambridge University Press, 2013.

Cocksworth, Ashley. *Karl Barth on Prayer*. London: Bloomsbury T&T Clark, 2015.

———. *Prayer: A Guide for the Perplexed*. London: Bloomsbury, 2018.

———. "When Prayer Goes Wrong: A Negative Theology of Prayer." *Scottish Journal of Theology* 76, no. 1 (2023): 10–23.

Cocksworth, Ashley, and John C. McDowell, eds. *The T&T Clark Handbook of Christian Prayer*. London: Bloomsbury, 2021.

Cocksworth, Ashley, and W. Travis McMaken, eds. *Karl Barth: Spiritual Writings*. Classics of Western Spirituality. New York: Paulist Press, 2022.

Cocksworth, Ashley, Rachel Starr, and Stephen Burns, eds. *From the Shores of Silence: Conversations in Feminist Practical Theology*. London: SCM, 2023.

Colón-Emeric, Edgardo. "*Vivens Pauper*: An Exploration of the Good Life with Óscar Romero." In *Exploring the Glory of God: New Horizons for a Theology of Glory*, edited by Adesola Joan Akala, 97–109. Lanham, MD: Rowman & Littlefield, 2021.

Crawley, Ashon T. *Blackpentecostal Breath: The Aesthetics of Possibility*. New York: Fordham University Press, 2016.

Culp, Kristine A. *Vulnerability and Glory: A Theological Account*. Louisville: Westminster John Knox, 2010.

Daly-Denton, Margaret. *David in the Fourth Gospel: The Johannine Reception of the Psalms*. Leiden: Brill, 2000.

Dante Alighieri. *The Divine Comedy: Inferno, Purgatorio, Paradiso*. Translated by Robin Kirkpatrick. London: Penguin, 2014.

Davis, Ellen F. *Opening Israel's Scriptures*. Oxford: Oxford University Press, 2019.

Davis, Ellen F., and Makoto Fujimura, with Shai Held. *Light within Light: Psalms and the Arts of Insight*. Waco: Baylor University Press, forthcoming.

Day, Abby. *The Religious Lives of Older Laywomen: The Last Active Anglican Generation*. Oxford: Oxford University Press, 2017.

Deane-Drummond, Celia. *Eco-Theology*. London: Darton, Longman & Todd, 2008.

Duchenne de Boulogne, G.-B. *The Mechanism of Human Facial Expression*. Edited and translated by R. Andrew Cuthbertson. Cambridge: Cambridge University Press, 1990.

Edwards, Jonathan. *The Works of Jonathan Edwards*. Vol. 13, *The "Miscellanies."* Edited by Thomas A. Schafer. New Haven: Yale University Press, 1994.

Ekman, Paul. "Duchenne and Facial Expression of Emotion." In *The Mechanism of Human Facial Expression*, by G.-B. Duchenne de Boulogne, edited and translated by R. Andrew Cuthbertson, 270–84. Cambridge: Cambridge University Press, 1990.

Fesko, John. *Beyond Calvin: Union with Christ and Justification in Early Modern Reformed Theology (1517–1700)*. Göttingen: Vandenhoeck & Ruprecht, 2012.

Florensky, Pavel. *The Pillar and Ground of the Truth: An Essay in Orthodox Theodicy in Twelve Letters*. Princeton: Princeton University Press, 2018.

Ford, David F. *Christian Wisdom: Desiring God and Learning in Love*. Cambridge: Cambridge University Press, 2007.

———. "The Desire of Jesus, Deep and Daring: What if . . ." In *God's Church for God's World: Lambeth 2022 and the Anglican Communion*, edited by James Hawkey. London: SPCK, forthcoming.

———. *The Future of Christian Theology*. Oxford: Wiley-Blackwell, 2011.

———. *The Gospel of John: A Theological Commentary*. Grand Rapids: Baker Academic, 2022.

———. "Mature Ecumenism's Daring Future: Learning from the Gospel of John for the Twenty-First Century." In *Receptive Ecumenism as Transformative Ecclesial Learning: Walking the Way to a Church Re-formed*, edited by Paul D. Murray, Gregory A. Ryan, and Paul Lakeland, 414–28. Oxford: Oxford University Press, 2022.

———. "Reading Backwards, Reading Forwards, and Abiding: Reading John in the Spirit Now." *Journal of Theological Interpretation* 2, no. 1 (2017): 69–84.

———. *Self and Salvation: Being Transformed*. Cambridge: Cambridge University Press, 1999.

———. *The Shape of Living: Spiritual Directions for Everyday Life*. Norwich: Canterbury Press, 2012.

———. "'To See My Glory': Jesus and the Dynamics of Glory in John's Gospel." In *Exploring the Glory of God: New Horizons for a Theology of Glory*, edited by Adesola Joan Akala, 15–26. Lanham, MD: Rowman & Littlefield, 2021.

————. "Ultimate Desire: The Prayer of Jesus in John 17." In *The T&T Clark Handbook of Christian Prayer*, edited by Ashley Cocksworth and John C. McDowell, 103–19. London: Bloomsbury, 2021.

Ford, David F., and Daniel W. Hardy. *Living in Praise: Worshipping and Knowing God*. London: Darton, Longman & Todd, 2005. The second edition of Hardy and Ford, *Jubilate*.

Ford, David F., Deborah Hardy Ford, and Ian Randall, eds. *A Kind of Upside-Downness: Learning Disabilities and Transformational Community*. London: Jessica Kingsley Publishers, 2020.

Fout, Jason A. *Fully Alive: The Glory of God and the Human Creature in Karl Barth, Hans Urs von Balthasar and Theological Exegesis of Scripture*. London: Bloomsbury, 2015.

Goshen-Gottstein, Alon. *In God's Presence: A Theological Reintroduction to Judaism*. Minneapolis: Fortress, 2023.

Greggs, Tom. *Dogmatic Ecclesiology*. Vol. 1, *The Priestly Catholicity of the Church*. Grand Rapids: Baker Academic, 2019.

————. "The Glory of God in the People of God: Participating in the Intensity of the Spirit's Life." In *Exploring the Glory of God: New Horizons for a Theology of Glory*, edited by Adesola Joan Akala, 37–53. Lanham, MD: Rowman & Littlefield, 2021.

Gregory of Nazianzus. *Gregoire de Nazianze: Discours 42–43*. Edited by Jean Bernardi. Sources chrétiennes 384. Paris: Cerf, 1992.

————. "On the Holy Spirit." In *St. Cyril of Jerusalem: Catechetical Lectures; St. Gregory Nazianzen: Orations, Sermons, Letters, Prolegomena*. Nicene and Post-Nicene Fathers, Series 2, 7:318–28. Edinburgh: T&T Clark, 1980.

Gregory of Nyssa. *The Life of Moses*. Translated by Abraham J. Malherbe and Everett Ferguson. Classics of Western Spirituality. New York: Paulist Press, 1978.

Griffiths, Paul J. *Religious Reading: The Place of Reading in the Practice of Religion*. Oxford: Oxford University Press, 1999.

Hardy, Daniel W. *Wording a Radiance: Parting Conversations about God and the Church*. London: SCM, 2014.

Hardy, Daniel W., and David F. Ford. *Jubilate: Theology in Praise*. London: Darton, Longman & Todd, 1984.

————. *Praising and Knowing God*. Philadelphia: Westminster, 1985. The American edition of Hardy and Ford, *Jubilate*.

Hawkins, Peter S. "All Smiles: Poetry and Theology in Dante's *Commedia*." In *Dante's* Commedia: *Theology as Poetry*, edited by Vittorio Montemaggi and Matthew Treherne, 36–59. Notre Dame: University of Notre Dame Press, 2010.

Hays, Richard B. *Echoes of Scripture in the Gospels*. Waco: Baylor University Press, 2016.

Higton, Mike. *The Life of Christian Doctrine*. London: Bloomsbury, 2020.

———. *A Theology of Higher Education*. Oxford: Oxford University Press, 2010.

Higton, Mike, and Rachel Muers. *The Text in Play: Experiments in Reading Scripture*. Eugene, OR: Cascade Books, 2012.

Holmes, Barbara A. *Joy Unspeakable: Contemplative Practices of the Black Church*. Minneapolis: Fortress, 2017.

Hull, John M. *The Tactile Heart: Reflections on Theology and Blindness*. London: SCM, 2013.

———. *Touching the Rock: An Experience of Blindness*. London: SPCK, 1990.

Hunt, Stephen. *Rewriting the Feeding of the Five Thousand: John 6:1–15 as a Test Case for Johannine Dependence on the Synoptic Gospels*. New York: Lang, 2011.

Illich, Ivan. *In the Vineyard of the Text: A Commentary to Hugh's "Didascalicon."* Chicago: University of Chicago Press, 1996.

Irenaeus. *Against Heresies*. In *The Apostolic Fathers with Justin Martyr and Irenaeus*, vol. 1 of *The Ante-Nicene Fathers*. Edinburgh: T&T Clark, 1993.

Jennings, Willie James. *Acts*. Belief: A Theological Commentary on the Bible. Louisville: Westminster John Knox, 2017.

———. *After Whiteness: An Education in Belonging*. Grand Rapids: Eerdmans, 2020.

Julian of Norwich. *Showings*. Edited by Edmund Colledge and James Walsh. Classics of Western Spirituality. New York: Paulist Press, 1978.

Jüngel, Eberhard. *God as the Mystery of the World: On the Foundation of the Theology of the Crucified One in the Dispute between Theism and Atheism*. Translated by Darrell L. Guder. London: Bloomsbury, 2014.

Kasper, Walter. *A Handbook of Spiritual Ecumenism*. Hyde Park, NY: New City, 2007.

Kelsey, David H. *Human Anguish and God's Power*. Cambridge: Cambridge University Press, 2020.

Kilby, Karen. *God, Evil and the Limits of Theology*. London: Bloomsbury, 2020.

Lash, Nicholas. *Believing Three Ways in One God: A Reading of the Apostles' Creed*. London: SCM, 1992.

Leclercq, Jean. *The Love of Learning and the Desire for God: A Study of Monastic Culture*. New York: Fordham University Press, 1961.

Lee, Dorothy A. *Flesh and Glory: Symbolism, Gender, and Theology in the Gospel of John*. New York: Crossroad, 2002.

Leigh, Robert. "The Energetics of Attraction: Daniel Hardy's Theological Imagination, Sociopoiesis, and the Measurement of Scriptural Reasoning." *Journal of Scriptural Reasoning* 19, no. 1 (2020), https://jsr.shanti.virginia.edu/back-issues/vol-17-no-1-august-2018-special-issue-on-re-enchantment-and-scriptural-reasoning/the-energetics-of-attraction-daniel-hardys-theological-imagination-sociopoiesis-and-the-measurement-of-scriptural-reasoning/.

———. *Freedom and Flourishing: Being, Act, and Knowledge in Karl Barth's "Church Dogmatics."* Eugene, OR: Wipf & Stock, 2017.

Luther, Martin. *Heidelberg Disputation* (1518). In *Career of the Reformer I*, edited by Harold J. Grimm, 39–58. Luther's Works 31. Minneapolis: Augsburg, 1957.

———. *Lectures on Galatians.* Edited by Jaroslav Jan Pelikan. Luther's Works 27. St. Louis: Concordia, 1964.

Mathewes, Charles. "Some Remarks on Joy." *Journal of Positive Psychology* 15, no. 1 (2020): 95–98.

———. "Toward a Theology of Joy." In *Joy and Human Flourishing: Essays on Theology, Culture, and the Good Life,* edited by Miroslav Volf and Justin E. Crisp, 63–95. Minneapolis: Fortress, 2015.

May, Melanie A. *A Body Knows: A Theopoetics of Death and Resurrection.* London: Continuum, 1995.

McCabe, Herbert. *God Matters.* London: Continuum, 2005.

McFadyen, Alistair. *Bound to Sin: Abuse, Holocaust and the Christian Doctrine of Sin.* Cambridge: Cambridge University Press, 2000.

———. "Imaging God: A Theological Answer to the Anthropological Question?" *Zygon* 47, no. 4 (2012): 918–33.

Messinger, Daniel, and Jacquelyn Moffitt. "Smiling." In *Encyclopedia of Infant and Early Childhood Development,* edited by Janette B. Benson, 157–72. 2nd ed. Amsterdam: Elsevier, 2020.

Moltmann, Jürgen. "Christianity: A Religion of Joy." In *Joy and Human Flourishing: Essays on Theology, Culture, and the Good Life,* edited by Miroslav Volf and Justin E. Crisp, 1–16. Minneapolis: Fortress, 2015.

———. *The Coming of God: Christian Eschatology.* London: SCM, 1996.

Morgan, Michael L. *The Cambridge Introduction to Emmanuel Levinas.* Cambridge: Cambridge University Press, 2011.

Moschella, Mary Clark. *Caring for Joy: Narrative, Theology, and Practice.* Leiden: Brill, 2016.

Muers, Rachel. "Creatures." In *Systematic Theology and Climate Change,* edited by Peter Scott and Michael Northcott, 90–107. London: Routledge, 2014.

Muers, Rachel, and Ashley Cocksworth with David F. Ford, eds. *Ford's The Modern Theologians: An Introduction to Christian Theology since 1918*. 4th ed. Oxford: Wiley, forthcoming.

Murray, Paul D. "Introducing Receptive Ecumenism." *The Ecumenist* 51, no. 2 (2014): 1–8.

Murray, Paul D., Gregory A. Ryan, and Paul Lakeland, eds. *Receptive Ecumenism as Ecclesial Learning: Principles, Practices, and Perspectives*. Oxford: Oxford University Press, 2022.

Ochs, Peter. "Morning Prayer as Redemptive Thinking." In *Liturgy, Time, and the Politics of Redemption*, edited by Randi Rashkover and C. C. Pecknold, 50–87. Grand Rapids: Eerdmans, 2006.

———. *Religion without Violence: The Practice and Philosophy of Scriptural Reasoning*. Eugene, OR: Cascade Books, 2019.

O'Donnell, Karen. *Broken Bodies: The Eucharist, Mary and the Body in Trauma Theology*. London: SCM, 2018.

———. *Survival: Radical Spiritual Practices for Trauma Survivors*. London: SCM, forthcoming.

O'Siadhail, Micheal. *Testament*. Waco: Baylor University Press, 2022.

Pattison, Stephen. *Saving Face: Enfacement, Shame, Theology*. London: Routledge, 2016.

Pizzey, Antonia. *Receptive Ecumenism and the Renewal of the Ecumenical Movement: The Path of Ecclesial Conversion*. Leiden: Brill, 2019.

Quash, Ben. *Found Theology: History, Imagination and the Spirit*. London: Bloomsbury, 2014.

Rambo, Shelly. *Spirit and Trauma: A Theology of Remaining*. Louisville: Westminster John Knox, 2010.

Ramsey, Michael. *The Glory of God and the Transfiguration of Christ*. London: Darton, Longman & Todd, 1967.

Rivera, Mayra. "Glory: The First Passion of Theology?" In *Polydoxy: Theology of Multiplicity and Relation*, edited by Catherine Keller and Laurel Schneider, 167–81. New York: Routledge, 2010.

Rogers, Eugene F. *After the Spirit: A Constructive Pneumatology from Resources outside the Modern West*. London: SCM, 2006.

Root, Andrew. *The Congregation in a Secular Age: Keeping Sacred Time against the Speed of Modern Life*. Grand Rapids: Baker Academic, 2021.

Rosa, Hartmut. *Resonance: A Sociology of Our Relationship to the World*. London: Polity, 2019.

———. *The Uncontrollability of the World*. Oxford: Wiley, 2020.

Sanders, Barry. *Sudden Glory: Laughter as Subversive History*. Boston: Beacon, 1995.

Sanders, Cheryl J. *Saints in Exile: The Holiness-Pentecostal Experience in African American Religion and Culture*. Oxford: Oxford University Press, 1999.

Shakespeare, Steven. *The Earth Cries Glory: Daily Prayer with Creation*. London: SCM, 2019.

Slee, Nicola. *Fragments for Fractured Times: What Feminist Practical Theology Brings to the Table*. London: SCM, 2020.

Sonderegger, Katherine. *Systematic Theology*. Vol. 1, *The Doctrine of God*. Minneapolis: Fortress, 2015.

———. *Systematic Theology*. Vol. 2, *The Doctrine of the Holy Trinity: Processions and Persons*. Minneapolis: Fortress, 2020.

Southgate, Christopher. *Theology in a Suffering World: Glory and Longing*. Cambridge: Cambridge University Press, 2018.

Starkenburg, Keith. "No Cowering Down: Glory, Election and Worship in Karl Barth's Doctrine of God." In *Exploring the Glory of God: New Horizons for a Theology of Glory*, edited by Adesola Joan Akala, 65–79. Lanham, MD: Rowman & Littlefield, 2021.

Steiner, George. *After Babel: Aspects of Language and Translation*. Oxford: Oxford University Press, 1975.

Tanner, Kathryn. *Christ the Key*. Cambridge: Cambridge University Press, 2009.

Thomas, Gabrielle. "The Cappadocians on the Beauty and Efficacy of Prayer." In *The T&T Clark Handbook to Christian Prayer*, edited by Ashley Cocksworth and John C. McDowell, 287–301. London: T&T Clark, 2021.

———. *For the Good of the Church: Unity, Theology and Women*. London: SCM, 2021.

Ticciati, Susannah. *Job and the Disruption of Identity: Reading beyond Barth*. London: T&T Clark, 2005.

Tonstad, Linn. *God and Difference: The Trinity, Sexuality, and the Transformation of Finitude*. London: Routledge, 2015.

Traherne, Thomas. *The Works of Thomas Traherne*. Vol. 2, *Commentaries of Heaven, Part 1: Abhorrence to Alone*. Edited by Jan Ross. Martlesham: Boydell & Brewer, 2007.

———. *The Works of Thomas Traherne*. Vol. 3, *Commentaries of Heaven, Part 2: Al-Sufficient to Bastard*. Edited by Jan Ross. Martlesham: Boydell & Brewer, 2007.

Ward, Graham. *How the Light Gets In: Ethical Life I*. Oxford: Oxford University Press, 2018.

Watkins, Clare. *Disclosing Church: An Ecclesiology Learned from Conversations in Practice*. London: Routledge, 2020.

Webster, John. *Holiness*. London: SCM, 2003.

Wells, Samuel, and Sarah Coakley, eds. *Praying for England: Priestly Presence in Contemporary Culture*. London: Continuum, 2008.

White, Lynn. "Continuing the Conversation." In *Western Man and Environmental Ethics: Attitudes toward Nature and Technology*, edited by Ian G. Barbour, 55–64. Boston: Addison-Wesley, 1953.

Williams, Rowan. *Arius: Heresy and Tradition*. London: SCM, 2001.

———. *Tokens of Trust: An Introduction to Christian Belief*. Norwich: Canterbury Press, 2007.

Wright, Kenneth. *Vision and Separation: Between Mother and Baby*. London: Free Association Books, 1991.

Wright, N. T. *History and Eschatology: Jesus and the Promise of Natural Theology*. London: SPCK, 2019.

Young, Frances M. *The Making of the Creeds*. London: SCM, 2015.

———. *Scripture, the Genesis of Doctrine*. Vol. 1 of *Doctrine and Scripture in Early Christianity*. Grand Rapids: Eerdmans, 2023.

Zahl, Simeon. *The Holy Spirit and Christian Experience*. Oxford: Oxford University Press, 2020.

Scripture Index

153

Subject Index